HARPENDEN

A VILLAGE IN WARTIME

To Peter
With best wishes,
John Cooper.
12/10/18

JOHN COOPER

AMBERLEY

Dedicated to the memory of
my dear friend Jack Richardson
13/10/1944 – 03/02/2018

ALSO BY JOHN COOPER

A Harpenden Childhood Remembered: Growing Up in the 1940s & '50s
Making Ends Meet: A Working Life Remembered
A Postcard From Harpenden: A Nostalgic Glimpse of the Village Then and Now
Watford Through Time
A Postcard From Watford
Harpenden Through Time
Rickmansworth, Croxley Green & Chorleywood Through Time
Hertfordshire's Historic Inland Waterway: Batchworth to Berkhamsted
Harpenden: The Postcard Collection
Watford History Tour

First published 2018

Amberley Publishing
The Hill, Stroud
Gloucestershire, GL5 4EP

www.amberley-books.com

British Library Cataloguing in Publication Data.

A catalogue record for this book is available from the British Library.

ISBN 978 1 4456 8905 0 (print)
ISBN 978 1 4456 8906 7 (ebook)

Origination by Amberley Publishing.
Printed in the UK.

Contents

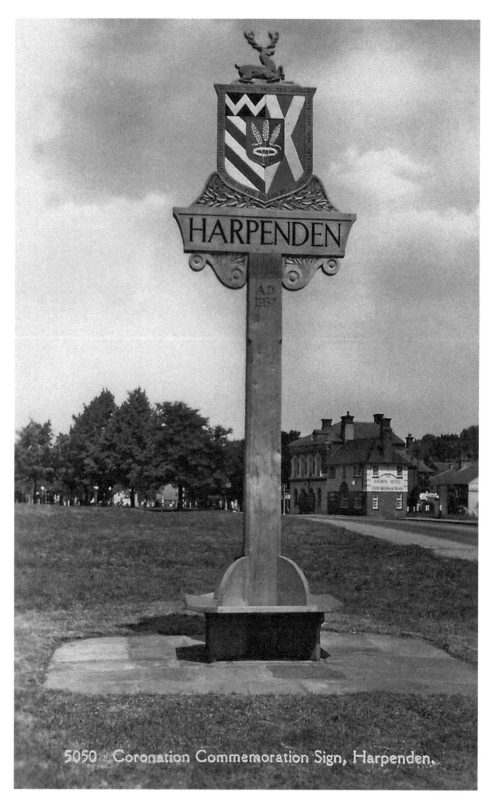

5050 Coronation Commemoration Sign, Harpenden.

Introduction

Harpenden: A Village in Wartime takes the reader on a fascinating journey that covers the first half of the twentieth century, a time of great change and expansion in this lovely Hertfordshire village.

Following the assassination of Archduke Franz Ferdinand of Austria in Sarajevo on 28 June 1914, Europe was a tinderbox waiting to explode as one by one the major powers took up arms. The final spark that lit the fuse of war came when Germany invaded Belgium on the morning of 4 August, heralding the start of the bloody conflict that was the First World War.

We first witness the effect that this major event had on the community in Harpenden when over 4,000 troops were seconded to the area to carry out an extensive training programme prior to their eventual departure to the horrors of northern France.

The first contingent to arrive in the village on 21 August 1914 consisted of soldiers of the Notts & Derby Regiment, the Sherwood Foresters. In order to accommodate such a large number of people the men were billeted in houses and cottages in and around the locality, with public buildings requisitioned to serve as messes, and for administrative purposes.

With the signing of the Armistice on 11 November 1918, bringing to an end four years of hostilities, the interwar years of the 1920s and 1930s were a time of considerable growth in Harpenden as new housing estates were built and twenty-one roads were constructed. As peace and tranquillity gradually started to return to this picturesque part of Hertfordshire and people were beginning to get out and about again, a popular venue was the nearby Green Lawns, a small country club at Kinsbourne Green where the fashionable clientele could enjoy a quiet gourmet dinner or an energetic game of tennis.

Another favourite meeting place was Mary-Ellen's, a quintessentially English tearoom where the proprietor, Miss Helen Finnie, offered afternoon tea, scones and delicious home-made cakes to her many customers. Soon, though, these pleasant outings would be just a memory as rumbles of the forthcoming conflict with Nazi Germany drew ever closer.

As the storm clouds of the Second World War started to gather in the late 1930s, Harpenden prepared for the inevitable. During those months prior to that fateful September day, preparations had already started to be put in place in the event of invasion and aerial attack. These included digging trenches, the distribution of Anderson shelters, covering doors and windows to comply with blackout regulations, and sticking adhesive tape to the inside of windows as a protection in the event of a bomb blast, as well as the issue of gas masks.

As the war dragged on into its second year, the nocturnal visits to the air-raid shelters, coupled with rationing and severe shortages, formed a regular uninterrupted pattern in people's daily lives: the sounds of the sirens, rising and falling in a crescendo that put fear and dread into your whole body; leaving the comfort of one's bed and hurrying into the cold night air to the shelter in the garden or backyard; the deep throb of the turbo engines from the bombers passing overhead; and then eventually the relief of the 'all clear'.

Memories are also rekindled of several of the morale-boosting parades through the village by the local Home Guard in aid of 'War Savings Promotion Week' and 'Wings for Victory Week', and towards the end of the war the sight of German prisoners clearing the High Street of snow under the vigilance of an armed guard.

On Tuesday 8 May 1945, the long-awaited day that the whole country had prayed and longed for arrived – peacetime. This was Victory in Europe Day (VE Day), although it would be another three months before the war was finally over. When two hydrogen bombs were dropped on Hiroshima and Nagasaki, bringing victory with the war on Japan (VJ Day), nearly six years of hostilities had at last ended.

Following Prime Minister Winston Churchill's announcement that 8 May 1945 was designated a public holiday, people from all over the country, including Harpenden, came out onto the streets in joyous celebration. Church bells rang out, schools closed and there was a palpable buzz of excitement and happiness as the residents prepared their own festivities as, like numerous communities in and around the village, huge bonfires were swiftly erected.

During the drab post-war years of rationing and austerity two events brought some much-needed colour and excitement to the country, and especially Harpenden, with the 1951 Festival of Britain and the coronation of Elizabeth II in 1953, both occasions allowing the local residents to momentarily forget the deprivation and shortages that were still very much in evidence. It was sheer magic while it lasted.

Harpenden has seen and experienced much in almost forty years of war and peace as this quiet agricultural village gradually developed into the attractive town that we see today.

Chapter 1

Memories of the First World War

Following the assassination of Archduke Franz Ferdinand of Austria in Sarajevo on 28 June 1914, Europe was a tinderbox waiting to explode as one by one the major powers took up arms. The final spark that lit the fuse of war came when Germany invaded Belgium on the morning of 4 August, heralding the start of the bloody conflict that was the First World War – the 'war to end all wars'.

Once war had been declared, the Territorial Army was immediately mobilised. Hertfordshire was allocated as the training area for the North Midlands Division, which included the Notts & Derby and the Stafford Infantry brigades. The first contingent to arrive in Harpenden on 21 August 1914 consisted of around 4,000 troops of the Notts & Derby Regiment, the Sherwood Foresters.

In order to accommodate such a large number of people, soldiers were billeted in houses and cottages in and around the locality, with public buildings requisitioned to serve as messes, and for administrative purposes.

A considerable amount of the soldiers' activities took place on the Common, which included hand-to-hand combat, weaponry and physical training, all viewed with great interest by groups of local spectators on the periphery.

Local farmland, including Thrales End Farm to the north of Harpenden, was also utilised and the men learnt to cope with barbed wire entanglements. The order was then given for their departure to Harlow, Essex, on 16 November, where they were to dig a defensive trench system to counter a rumoured threat of invasion on the Essex coast prior to their eventual embarkation to France on 25 February 1915. A month earlier, battalions of the North and South Staffordshire regiments had arrived in Harpenden.

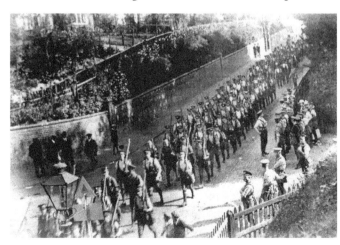

Troops of the Sherwood Foresters marching down Station Road following their arrival at Harpenden East station.

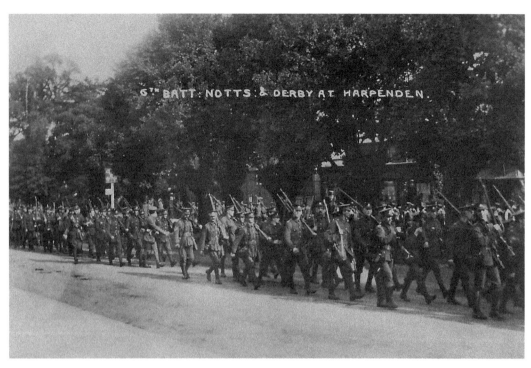

Sunday Church Service
Soldiers of the Notts & Derby marching along the High Street for a regimental service on the Common on Sunday 23 August 1914, shortly after their arrival.

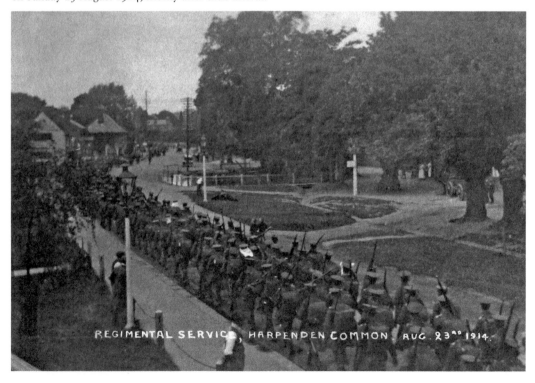

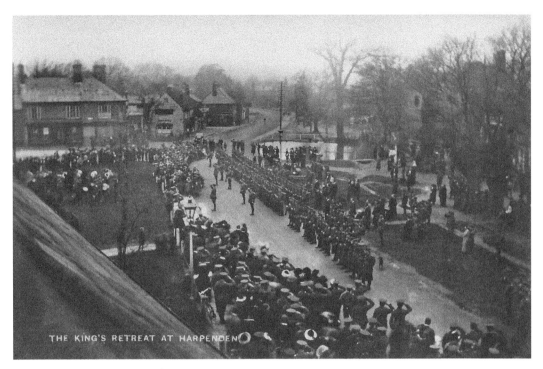

THE KING'S RETREAT AT HARPENDEN

The High Street 1914/15
Two iconic images that depict the high military presence that existed in Harpenden during the early months of the First World War.

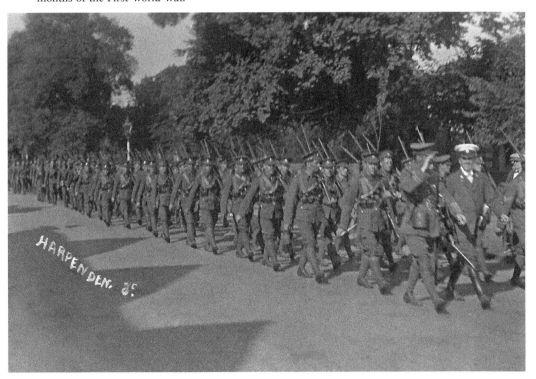

HARPENDEN.

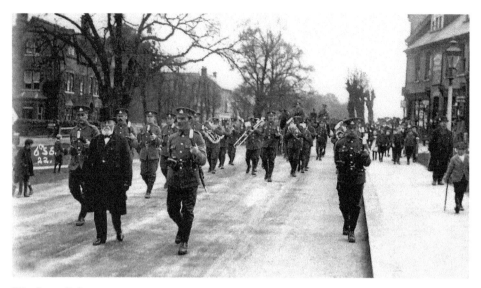

The Last Salute

A cold grey day in February 1915 as a military funeral, led by local undertaker Mr Frederick Piggott, proceeds sombrely along the High Street en route to St Nicholas's Churchyard where a young soldier of the North Staffordshire Regiment will be laid to rest with full military honours, having succumbed to influenza a few days earlier after a short illness. He was just seventeen, having only enlisted in the army two and a half months earlier. Soldiers from his company fired three volleys over the grave and buglers played 'The Last Post'. The Institute in Wheathampstead Road where the soldier had died had been requisitioned early in the war as a military hospital. However, as this facility had proved to be too small, Henry Tylston Hodgson of 'The Welcombe' offered his second home, No. 28 Milton Road, to the senior commanding army officer of the troops, rent free, for use as a more spacious hospital later in 1915. The inset image shows the same quiet corner of the churchyard today where there are fourteen military burials, mostly distinguishable by their Portland or Italian limestone headstones.

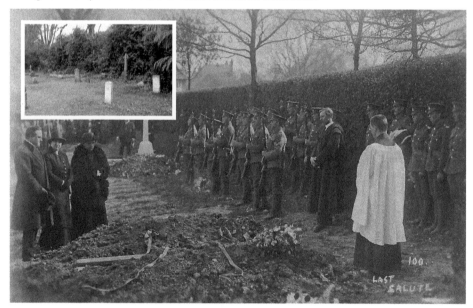

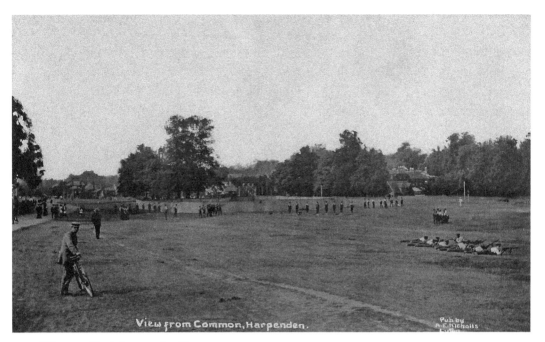

Weapon Training on the Common

On a sunny late summer's day in 1914 some bemused local residents were able to watch with interest soldiers of the Notts & Derby Regiment carrying out weapon training and fieldcraft on the Common in preparation for the conflict ahead. There was a short respite while the soldiers waited for a herd of cattle to disperse after ambling across the grass in front of them. The Silver Cup Pond in the background of the above picture had been screened off to give the men maximum privacy when taking their daily bathe.

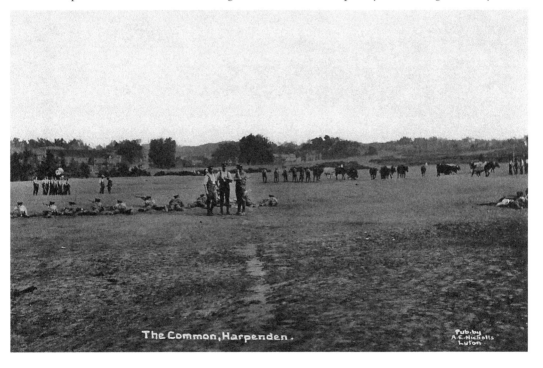

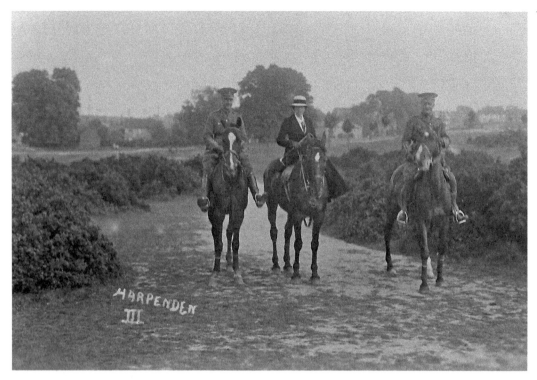

A Horse Ride on the Common

Portrayed in the unused postcard above are two officers who appear to be enjoying a quiet off-duty horse ride with a lady companion, who can be seen riding side-saddle. Just visible in the background is the Queen's Head public house and the Midland Railway in the Bowling Alley, South Harpenden. Below is a posed picture of what appears to be a company of non-commissioned officers and other ranks.

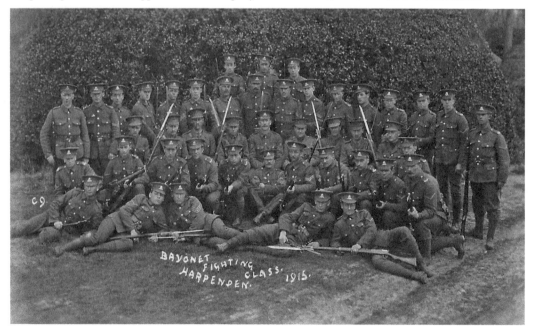

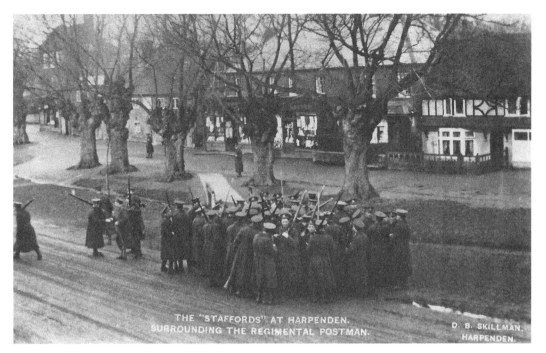

*THE "STAFFORDS" AT HARPENDEN.
SURROUNDING THE REGIMENTAL POSTMAN.*

*D. B. SKILLMAN,
HARPENDEN.*

Collecting the Mail

Above: An informal view of some of 'The Staffords' collecting their mail from the regimental postman in the High Street, just opposite Church Green. The soldiers were from the North and South Staffordshire regiments who arrived in Harpenden early in 1915.

Below: Another march as these soldiers are seen passing the Baa Lamb trees on the Common, with the Silver Cup public house just out of camera shot on the left.

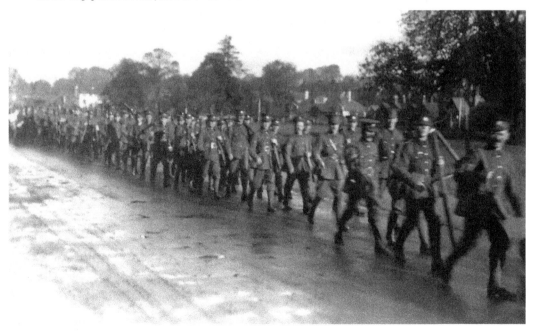

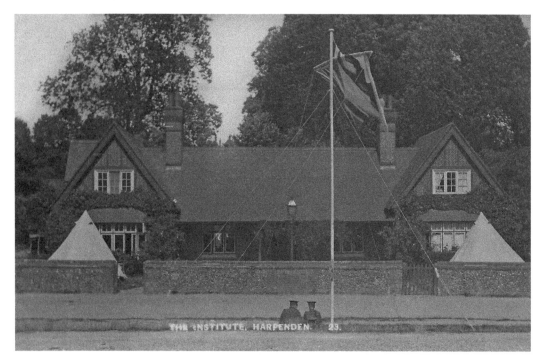

The Institute

Above: The Institute in Southdown Road was utilised as a military hospital during the early part of the First World War. It must have been in use for only a relatively short period of time during 1915, as records indicate that larger accommodation was provided later on that year in a house in Milton Road. Today the Institute is where the Religious Society of Friends – the Quakers – hold their meetings.

Below: A lone soldier on the Common showing the Institute, with the Red Cross flag and the two bell tents in front, just visible on the left of the picture.

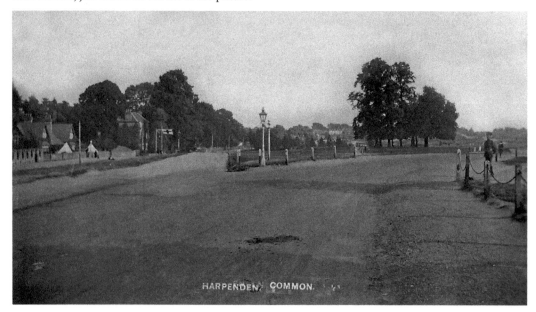

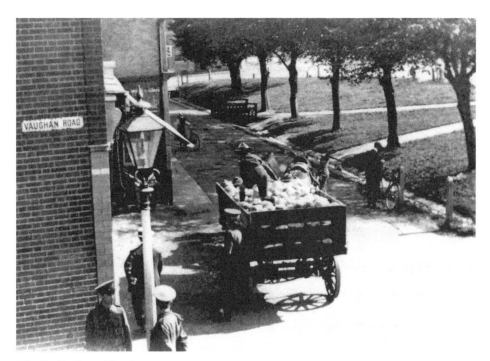

The Daily Bread Ration

While many soldiers had their meals where they were billeted, others ate at the various messes in the village. One of the many tasks that had to be carried out was to collect the daily bread ration from one of several local bakers. The one seen here is situated on the corner of Lower High Street and Vaughan Road. The loaves then had to be loaded onto a handcart that was trundled round to each mess, although the method of transport does not appear to be conducive to either hygiene or cleanliness.

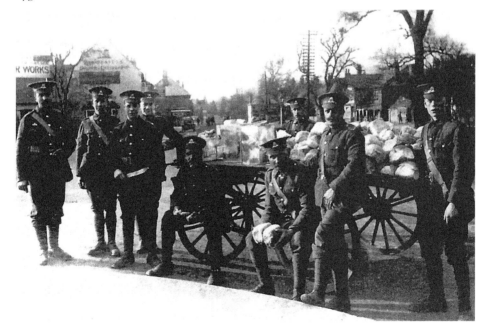

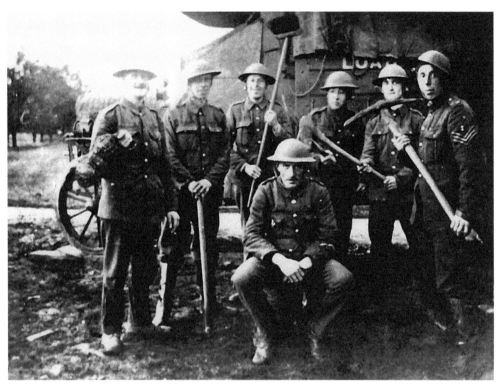

A Working Party Detail

Judging by the pickaxes and shovels these soldiers are carrying it is highly probable that this is a working party detail with orders to dig trenches, while the four off-duty brothers in arms posing for the camera below could well be standing in the road outside of their billet.

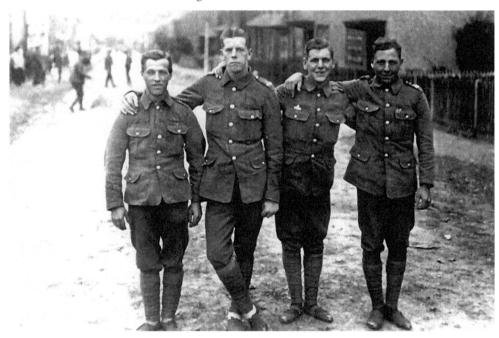

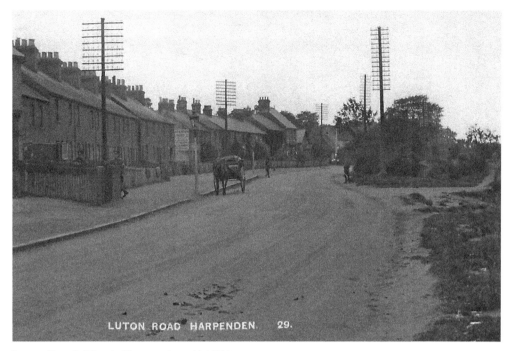

Luton Road, North Harpenden, 1914/15

The two soldiers seen chatting over the fence were either from the Notts & Derby or the Staffords, and more than likely were billeted in one of the cottages. With several thousand soldiers based in Harpenden during late 1914 and early 1915, they all had to be accommodated, which is why rooms were requisitioned from householders all over the village. The sign on the side of the house in Harpenden Rise is advertising 'Harpenden Laundry'. Bloomfield Road had yet to be built on the right-hand side. The picture below shows one of the many marquees that were erected on the Common following the soldiers' arrival, and was probably used as a mess tent.

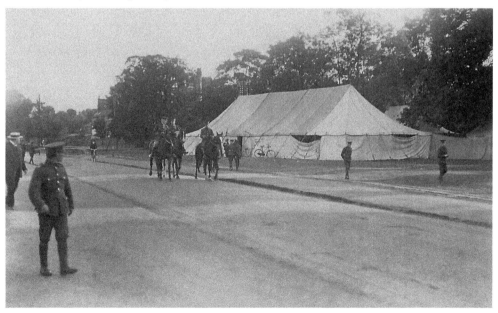

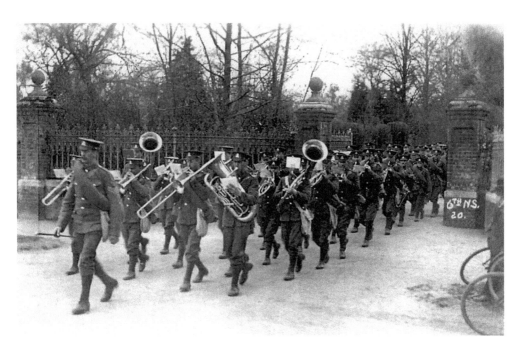

Inspection in Rothamsted Park

Following an inspection by the Earl of Dartmouth on 29 June 1915, the 6th North Staffordshire Battalion, led by their regimental band, is seen leaving Rothamsted Park where the earl had said that 'he had a very high opinion of the quality and soldierly bearing of the troops before him'.

The image below again shows the 6th North Staffs, marching along Leyton Road and approaching the entrance to Rothamsted Park, possibly for the same inspection.

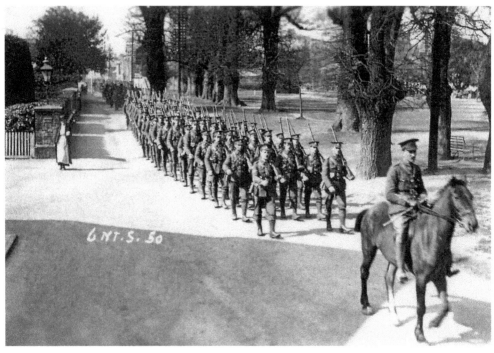

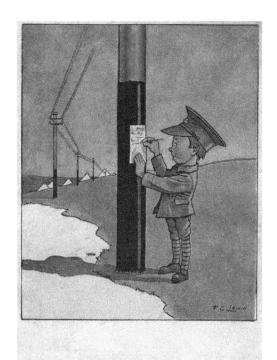

'I'm writing you
by the First Post!

Popular picture postcard images of the time.

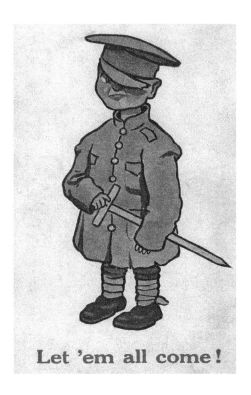

Let 'em all come!

Chapter 2
The Interwar Years

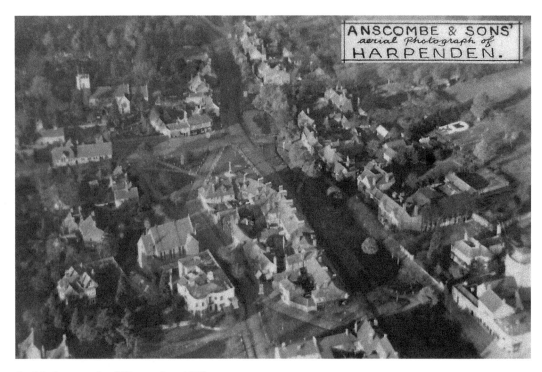

Aerial photograph of Harpenden, 1920.

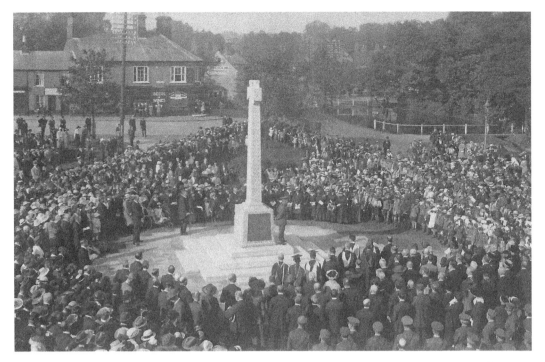

The War Memorial

Nearly two years after the signing of the armistice
that called for a ceasefire between the Allies and
Germany at 11 a.m. on 11 November 1918, bringing
to an end the hostilities of the First World War,
a momentous day took place in Harpenden on
Saturday 9 October 1920. This was the occasion
when the war memorial, dedicated to the local men
who had fought and died in the First World War
(1914–18) was unveiled at a special ceremony on
Church Green by Lieutenant-General Lord Cavan,
who had travelled the short distance from his home,
Wheathampstead House, in the nearby village of
Wheathampstead.

Many important dignitaries, as well as a large
crowd of people, had gathered to witness the historic
event. The names of the 164 men who had laid down
their lives are inscribed on two gunmetal tablets on
the granite Celtic wheel cross, with a further 110
names being added after the Second World War.
The cross is engraved on the front: 'To the Glorious
Memory of the Men of Harpenden who Fought
and Died in the Great War 1914–1918'. And on
the back: 'Erected by the People of Harpenden in
Gratitude, Love and Pride'.

Just over one month later, on 11 November
1920, the memorial was again the focus of attention
by the local populace as Remembrance Day was
recognised to honour the fallen, as seen below.

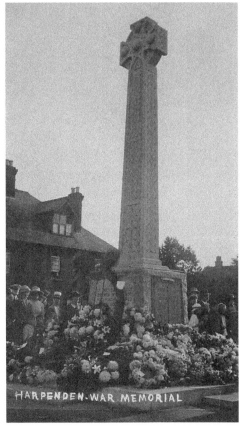

HARPENDEN·WAR·MEMORIAL

Now that the country was gradually getting back onto its feet again after four years of war, the 1920s and 1930s were a time of great expansion in Harpenden. Since 1920, 613 houses, thirty-one bungalows and thirty-four shops had been built, as well as the construction of twenty-one new roads. Farmlands between the High Street and Lower Luton Road were developed, as were the Roundwood and West Common areas.

With memories of the time in the early stages of the war when thousands of troops had been billeted around the village fast receding, peace and tranquillity started to return again to this picturesque part of Hertfordshire. Children paddled in the Silver Cup Pond, while many spectators enjoyed a lazy summer's afternoon of cricket on the Common.

A popular venue in the 1930s was the nearby Green Lawns at Kinsbourne Green, a small country club not far from Harpenden that attracted an elite and fashionable clientele who would motor out there to enjoy a quiet gourmet dinner or an energetic game of tennis. Another favourite meeting place was Mary-Ellen's, a genteel and quintessentially English tearoom in Leyton Road that opened in 1932. The proprietor, Miss Helen Finnie, offered afternoon tea, scones and delicious home-made cakes to her many customers.

Located a short distance away adjacent to the Silver Cup public house on the Common was Harry Bennett's coffee stall. This was a totally different eating establishment to Mary-Ellen's, catering for the basic needs of passing motorists and lorry drivers, where a mug of tea and a sandwich could be purchased for a modest price.

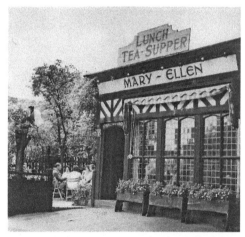

Mary-Ellen's.

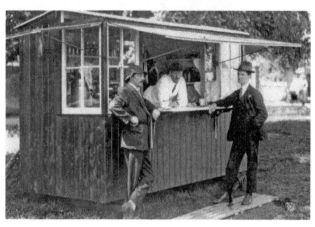

Harry Bennett's coffee stall.

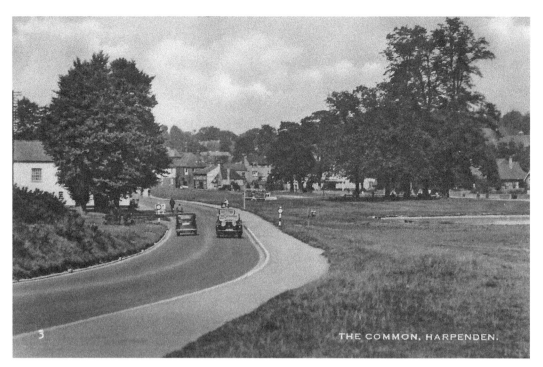

THE COMMON, HARPENDEN.

Motoring on the Common

This idyllic vista of the quiet main road across the Common and down into the village will before long be just a pleasant memory, as rumbles of the forthcoming conflict with Nazi Germany draw ever closer. These lovely old cars depicted in these two late 1930s postcards illustrate the time when motoring was a real pleasure. The Silver Cup pub is seen in the above photo on the left and the pond of the same name is on the right with the magnificent Baa Lamb trees, a local landmark, in the background.

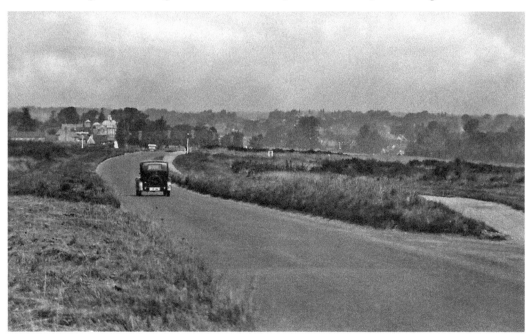

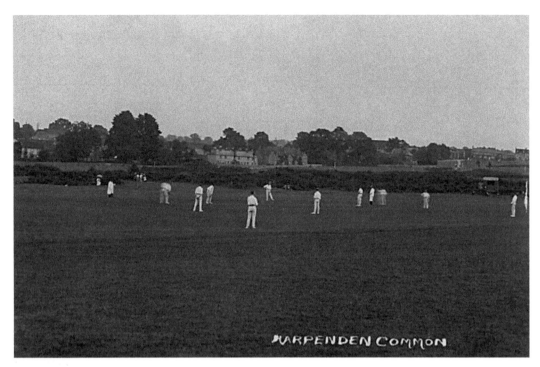

Harpenden Cricket Club

A warm summer's day in the 1920s, as some spectators watch a sociable and relaxing Sunday afternoon game of village cricket in this archetypal image taken on the Common. Harpenden Cricket Club was formed in 1863 when John Bennet Lawes, as lord of the manor and the club's first president, consented to the use of his 'wasteland' for cricket matches.

However, the first mention of cricket on the Common was over thirty years earlier when a game was played between four right-handed and four left-handed players. Unfortunately, the outcome of this 'novel match' was not recorded, but the odds were 6:4 on the left-handed batsmen. Throughout the 1920s and 1930s village cricket flourished on the Common, entertaining the many spectators as the sound of leather on willow could be heard in the peace and stillness of a sunny afternoon.

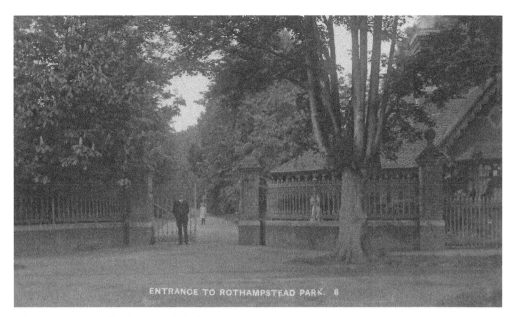

ENTRANCE TO ROTHAMPSTEAD PARK. 8

The Entrance to Rothamsted Park
Seen above in Leyton Road is the entrance and gates to Rothamsted Park, as depicted in a photo card that was posted on 15 August 1921. The park comprises a beautiful 56-acre area that was once part of the Rothamsted estate until it was purchased by the Urban District Council in 1938 as a place of relaxation and to provide sporting facilities. Today, the park is the location for the annual Harpenden Lions Highland Gathering, one of the largest Highland Games events outside Scotland.

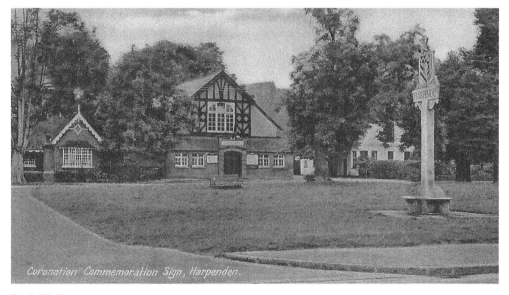

Coronation Commemoration Sign, Harpenden.

Park Hall
The historic building above, with its distinctive façade, is Park Hall. It was originally constructed in 1850 as a school and over the years has been used for council offices and a public hall. It is now available for community use and all types of functions, such as wedding receptions, dinner/dances and various exhibitions are held there. The town council offices are situated at the rear of the building. The 1937 Coronation Commemoration sign can be seen to the right of the picture.

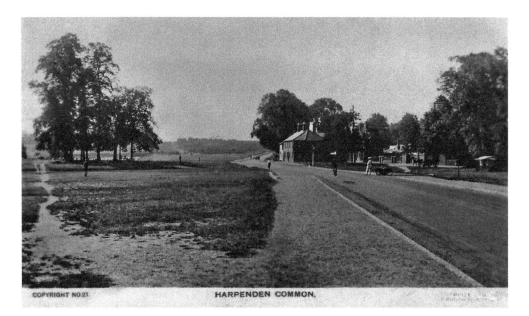

HARPENDEN COMMON.

Harpenden Common

This 1920s image shows what is now the busy A1081 but was then a quiet country road out of the village travelling in the direction of St Albans. The Baa Lamb trees on the Common can be seen on the left and some cottages and the Silver Cup public house are featured centrally. On the extreme right of the photo (with the white roof) is Harry Bennett's coffee stall.

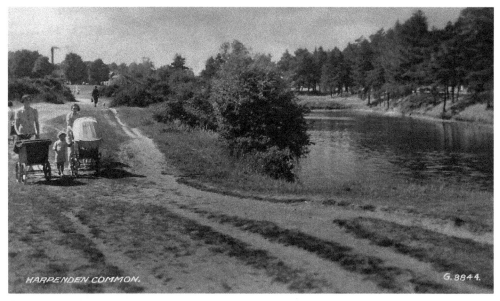

HARPENDEN COMMON. G.8844.

Prelude to War!

A lovely summer's day walk on the Common in the late 1930s. This card was sent on 12 August 1939, just over three weeks before the outbreak of the Second World War. The 'lake' was actually a drainage pond and, together with the many trees around its edge, was often known as 'Little Switzerland'. Although the area has now grown up considerably in the intervening years, it is nevertheless still a very pleasant place to enjoy an afternoon saunter.

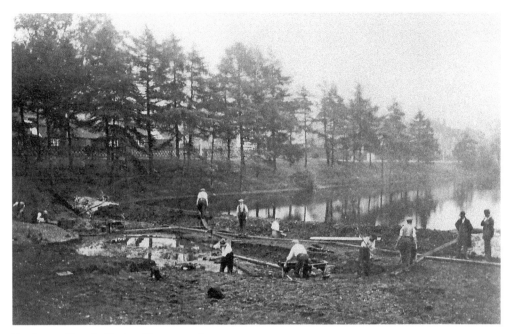

Drainage Ponds Under Construction

In 1928, the Urban District Council, following a review of its drainage system, decided to fill in the Cock Pond in the High Street and pipe the small stream that flowed along Lower High Street underground to the gravel pits on the Common adjacent to Southdown Road. This necessitated improving the pits as above, which had originally been dug out in the 1870s, to form three ponds at descending levels to take the storm and surface water from the village. The project was carried out around 1929 and provided much-needed work for the increasing number of unemployed in the area at that time. Today, this beautiful cool green oasis, sometimes known somewhat grandly as 'Little Switzerland', remains a pleasant place to stroll and linger awhile.

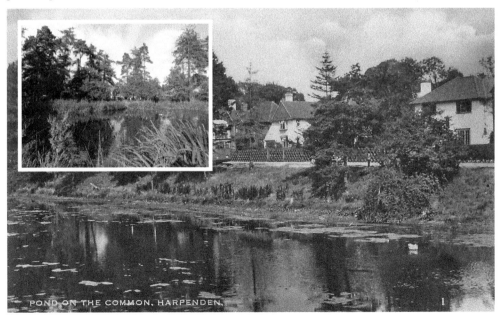

POND ON THE COMMON, HARPENDEN.

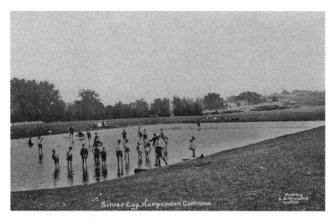

Silver Cup, Harpenden Common.

The Silver Cup Pond

The often-photographed Silver Cup Pond on the Common provided many a happy – and in all probability, very wet – hour or so spent either paddling or sailing a toy yacht to generations of youngsters who flocked to the water each summer. It was in 1899 that Sir John Bennet Lawes of Rothamsted Manor had the pond concreted from its natural state in order to provide a safer and more permanent environment for the countless children who used it. The middle image was taken around 1938, with the one at the top taken quite a number of years earlier. It was a sad day in 1970 when the pond was filled in and grassed over – it was deemed to be a potential health risk. The end of an era.

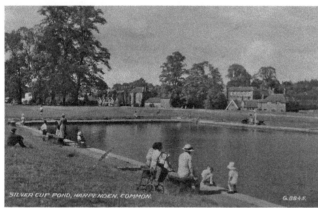

SILVER CUP POND, HARPENDEN. COMMON.   G.8645.

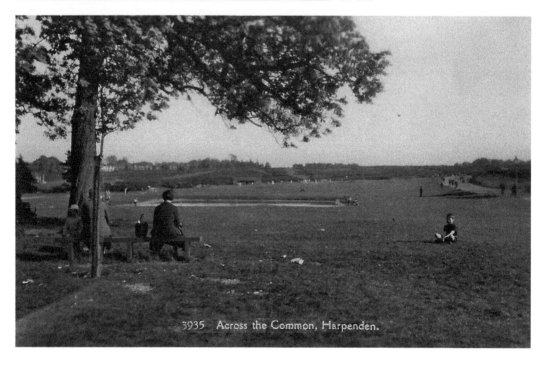

3935   Across the Common, Harpenden.

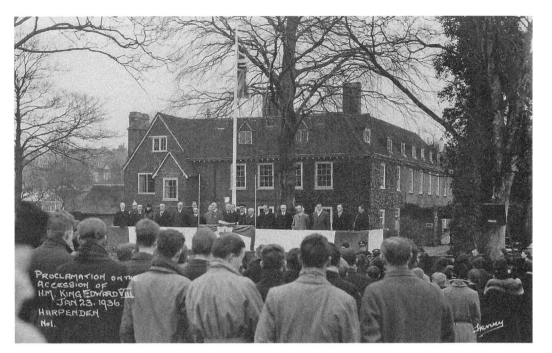

Harpenden Hall

Built in the sixteenth century, Harpenden Hall has seen many events in its long history including that in the above image, which captures the proclamation on the accession of Edward VIII on 23 January 1936. The hall was at one time a private asylum, a girls' boarding school and more recently the offices of the Urban District Council. From 1924 until 1931 the building was used by St Dominic's Convent School, until their move the short distance down Southdown Road to their new premises in the Welcombe, once the home of local benefactor Henry Tylston Hodgson.

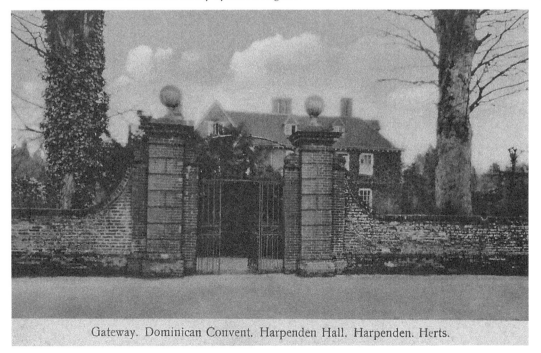

Gateway. Dominican Convent. Harpenden Hall. Harpenden. Herts.

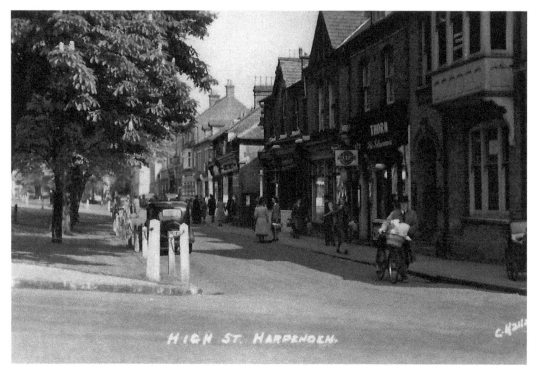

Lower High Street

These two lovely old postcards of Lower High Street were photographed from Station Road in the 1930s. The bottom photo particularly illustrates how Harpenden has a beauty and character all of its own, from the wide boulevard that is the High Street to the well-manicured greens.

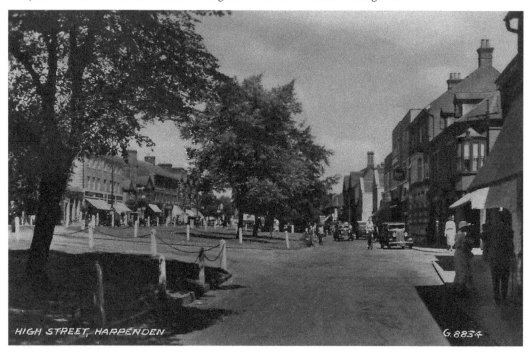

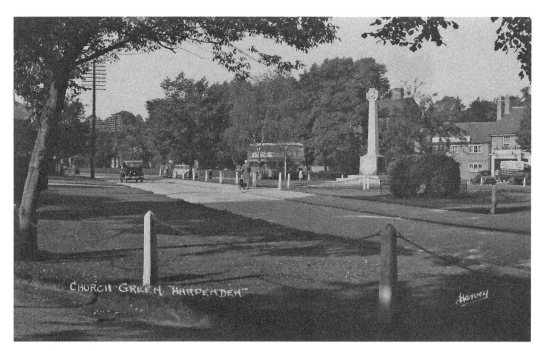

Church Green

Two delightful picture postcards, again from the 1930s, show picturesque views of the war memorial and the High Street, with the Cross Keys public house just visible in the background on the right-hand side of the top image. In the bottom photo, we look northwards across the Green towards the lovely parish church of St Nicholas, originally built in the thirteenth century as a chapel of ease to the mother church of St Helen's in Wheathampstead, remaining as such until 1859 when St Nicholas became a parish in its own right.

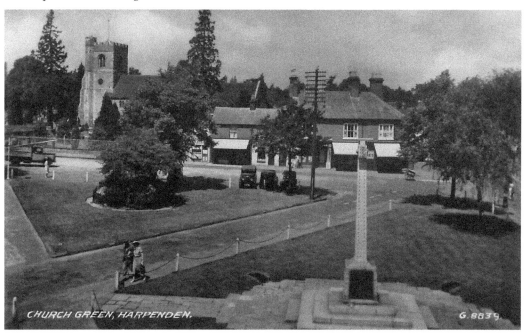

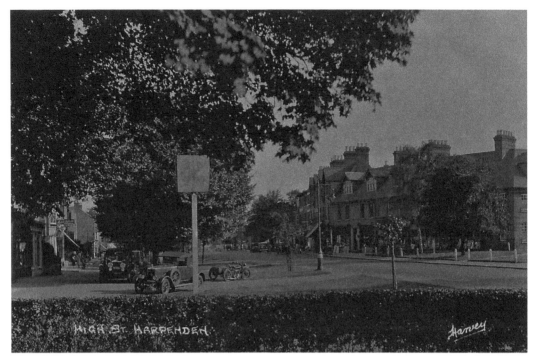

The Village Centre, Looking South

This delightful interwar postcard shows two lovely old automobiles parked outside the Cross Keys public house looking south along the High Street towards the Common. In 1890, the row of villas on the right was built occupying the island site between the High Street and Leyton Road, where there had previously been a large house and garden. Originally private homes, the villas, with their distinctive dormer windows facing Church Green and extending round the corner into the High Street, are today all shops with some flats above. The photo was taken where the Cock Pond used to be, which had been drained and grassed over in 1928.

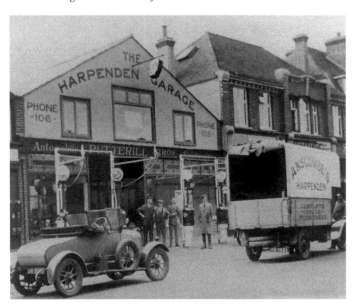

The Harpenden Garage – Putterill Bros

A charming image of Putterill Bros' Harpenden Garage, photographed in 1929/30, shows a delivery van from Anscombe's department store in Leyton Road. The front façade of the garage displays a very low telephone number, indicating that there were probably not too many subscribers in Harpenden at the time. Florence teashop can just be seen to the right of the picture and was still in existence in the early 1950s.

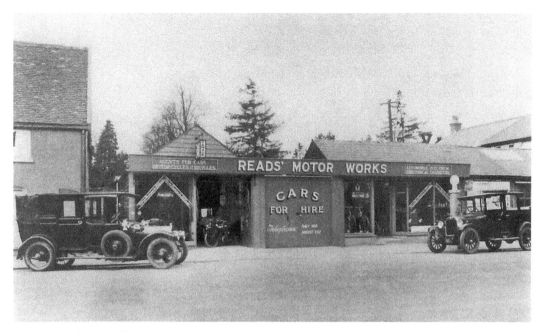

Reads' Motor Works

Reads' Motor Works at their High Street premises in the early 1920s, which was founded by Charles and William in 1921. They also occupied a site on Bowers Parade in the late 1930s where they had their showrooms. From their advertisement, Reads' also offered a high-quality range of perambulators and motorcycles in addition to a selection of luxury limousines and smaller family cars. In the wintry image below, part of a sign reading 'Motor Works' can just be made out, indicating this is where Reads' displayed their lovely, gleaming cars of the day.

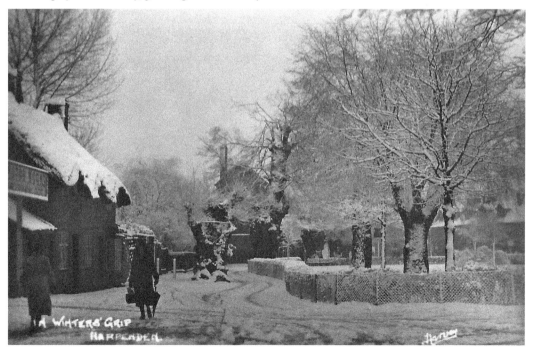

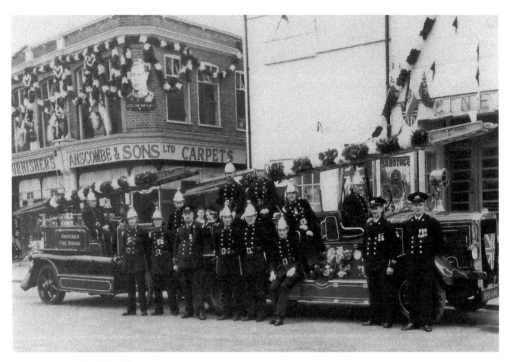

Coronation Celebrations

Harpenden Fire Brigade looking resplendent in their best uniforms, posing beside the brigade appliance outside the decorated frontage of Ancombe's, the village's most prestigious retail store, and the Regent Cinema in Leyton Road during the celebrations for the coronation of George VI on 12 May 1937.

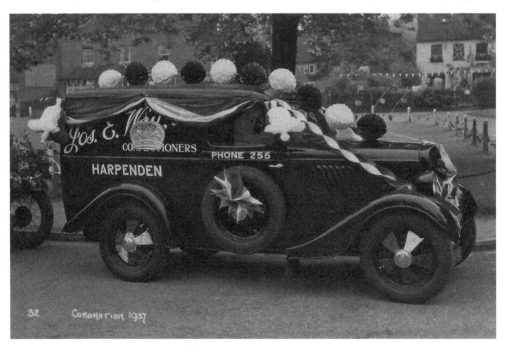

Local baker Joseph West in his decorated van that formed part of the carnival procession.

A Link with the Past

At the north end of the High Street, just before Sun Lane, is this lovely tranquil-looking walkway that photographer Cecil Hallam described as 'a link with the past', a truly apt description. The small building in the foreground, known as the Island Cottage, was at one time occupied by Fred Timson, 'Hand Sewn Bootmaker and Repairer'. The sender of this card writes, 'Overleaf is the little cobbler's shop, Timson's, where we have all had shoes repaired for over forty years. Timson himself has just retired after sixty years work in it. Love to all, your affectionate uncle Selwyn.' The picture postcard below depicts Sun Lane Cottage, which was drastically altered in the late 1920s when the northern end was demolished to facilitate the widening of Sun Lane.

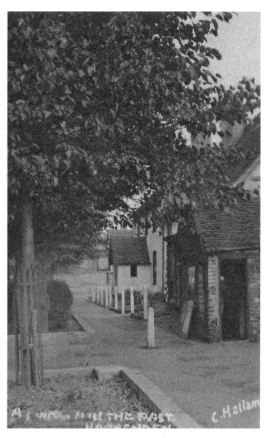

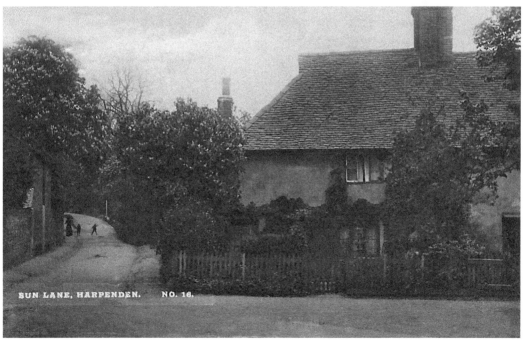

SUN LANE, HARPENDEN.   NO. 16.

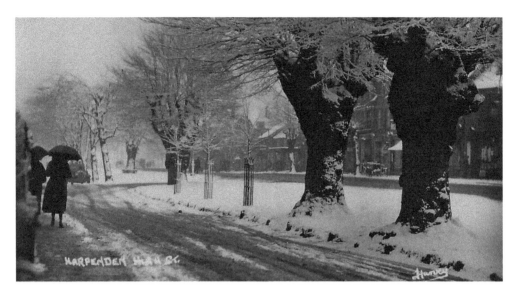

High Street

A picturesque winter's scene in Lower High Street during the 1930s. The small stream, grandly referred to as the River Harp, ran along the right-hand edge of the road from the Cock Pond. It was piped underground in the late 1920s, at the same time that the pond was filled in as part of an extensive new drainage system. An interesting anecdote was that in August 1879 following two hours of torrential rain, the village was flooded from Sun Lane to Wheathampstead Road when a daredevil gentleman, Jack Healy, who owned one of the two breweries in the village at that time, is reputed to have swum from the Cock Pond to the gravel pits on the Common and back – a magnificent feat that so far has supposedly never been repeated. It is not known whether a wager was involved!

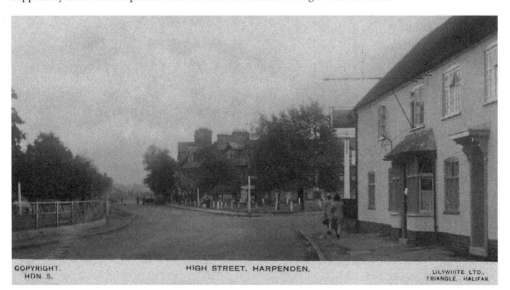

The Old Cock Inn and the High Street Looking South

The image above, which was franked on 6 August 1931, was probably photographed a few years earlier in the late 1920s. It shows a view of the High Street looking south with the Old Cock Inn in the foreground on the right. This would have been about the time that work would have commenced draining and filling the village pond opposite.

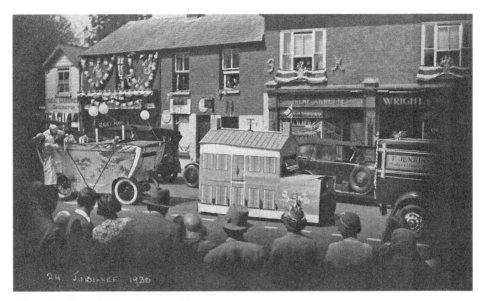

Silver Jubilee of King George V

Some of the spectators gathered along part of the route to watch the decorated floats and tableaux of the procession passing through Church Green to celebrate the Silver Jubilee of George V and Queen Mary in May 1935. In the background some of the various business premises can be seen decked out in red, white and blue bunting for the occasion, including those of George Gardner, decorator; Robert Sampson, fish dealer; Harold Bear, confectioner; 'Irene Annette', the hairdressing salon of Misses Bateman and Morgan; and just visible on the right, Wright & Mills, ophthalmic opticians.

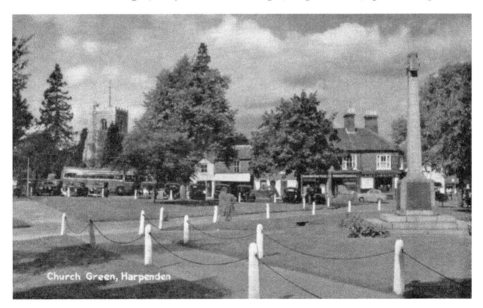

Church Green

A charming view of Church Green in the mid-1930s, where outwardly there appears to be very little change when compared to how it looks today, apart from the ongoing transition of shop ownership. Of course, today's aspect would encompass a mass of cars and vans, where parking nowadays in the village is always at a premium.

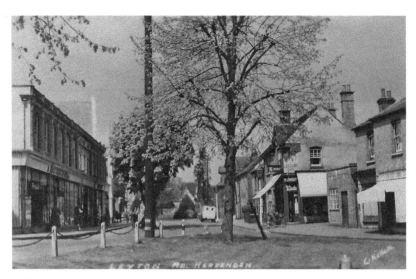

Anscombe's

Leyton Road looking north with Harpenden's most prestigious shop, Anscombe's, a store that exuded its own special brand of old-world charm, seen on the left of the top photo. It was founded in 1855 by Allen Anscombe, who started trading in a shop at the bottom of Thompson's Close. With the transfer of the business to Wellington House in 1874, the firm grew and over the years was extended along Leyton Road. The shop sold a variety of goods including haberdashery, linen, hosiery and menswear, as well as furniture.

A fascinating feature of the store was the overhead cash rail system called 'Rapid Wire', where money was catapulted in a container with a detachable cup across the shop on a wire to the cash desk. There the cashier would receipt the bill and return the container, together with any change, to the counter from where it had come. Meanwhile, the assistant had time to wrap the goods and possibly pass the time of day with the customer. Anscombe's closed in 1982 and a Waitrose supermarket now occupies the site.

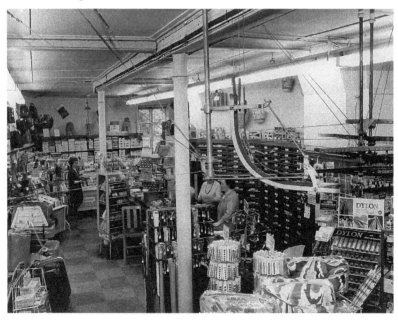

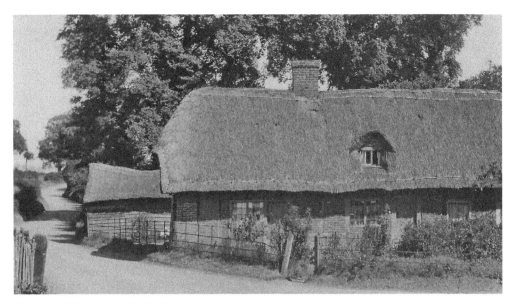

Thatched Cottages, Batford

A short distance from the Marquis of Granby pub across the River Lea near Batford Mill are the lovely old seventeenth-century thatched cottages, as featured in the above photo taken around 1925. There were originally three dwellings but they were amalgamated into one in 1958. Earlier occupants of the cottages included an agricultural worker and William 'Shep' Arnold, a local shepherd who lived there with his large family. Each day he herded his flock from Mackerye End Farm to the Common by way of Crabtree Lane. Life in the cottages at the turn of the nineteenth century was very hard and basic. There was no indoor sanitation and water for washing had to be drawn from the nearby river. A spring close by provided the drinking water.

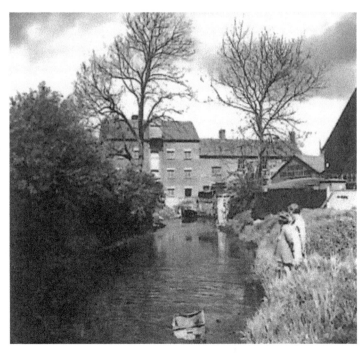

Batford Mill

Batford Mill, pictured in the late 1930s. The mill was one of four in the parish of Wheathampstead, which included Harpenden, mentioned in the Domesday Book of 1086. Today the old mill has been completely renovated and is occupied by offices and industrial units. There is little evidence now to show where the River Lea once flowed as it was diverted from its original course through the mill in 1954.

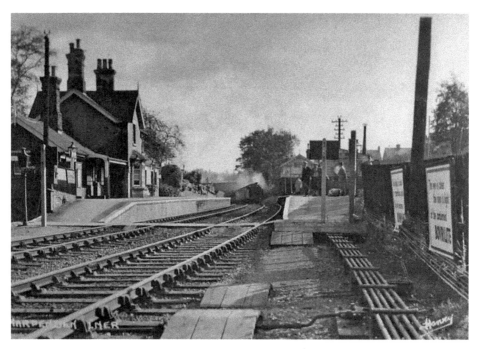

Harpenden East Station

Harpenden East station in the 1930s. The line ran from Dunstable to Hatfield and was opened in 1860, finally closing under the Beeching axe in 1965. During the Second World War the railway line was used to transport Churchill tanks that had been manufactured at Vauxhall Motors, Luton.

Waveney Road, a housing development, has now been built on the area where the old railway station once stood and where steam trains rattled along tracks long since removed. More than fifty years later, it is not uncommon for the keen gardeners in the road to dig up some of the crushed stone ballast that was once used to form the trackbed upon which the railway sleepers were laid.

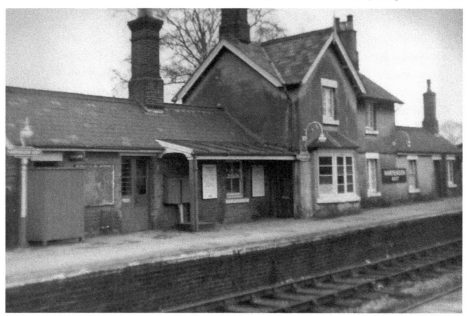

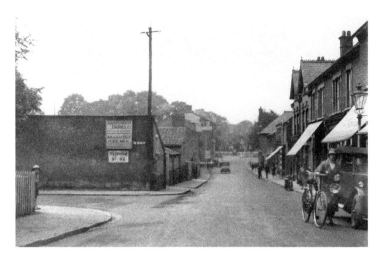

Station Road

Above: Over ninety years have elapsed since that Thursday in August 1927 when this snapshot of Station Road at the junction with Arden Grove was taken. From a quiet, peaceful thoroughfare in those calm traffic-free days, it is now a busy link to Batford in the east of the town. Back in 1927, the advertisement on the wall proclaims that this is the home of Harpenden Dairies, a thriving business run by its managing director, Frederick Norman Gingell, a popular and ebullient man who was also chairman of the Urban District Council. Next to the dairy was where the new post office would shortly be constructed and which opened in September 1928. The property on the opposite corner belonged to Henry Salisbury, a local builder, who lived there until his death in 1923 when the premises became a dental practice run by Arthur Renwick Lambie and Harold Wardill until 1956. The house was demolished in the early 1960s when the site was redeveloped as a row of shops forming Harding Parade.

Below: This 1920s postcard shows Station Road with Ridleys' ironmongery shop on the left-hand corner, a few years before its acquisition by the Midland Bank in 1933. The Benskins Brewery vehicle on the right of the picture could well have been making a delivery to the Railway Hotel, the large building in the foreground, now the Harpenden Arms, a prestigious pub and Thai restaurant. At one stage the Railway Hotel was the meeting place of the Ancient Order of Foresters, who held a grand fête once a year – then one of the most popular events in the village calendar.

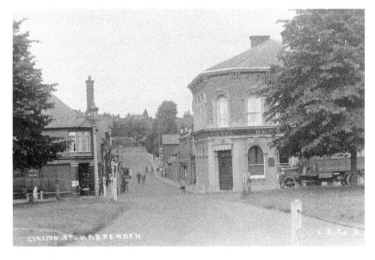

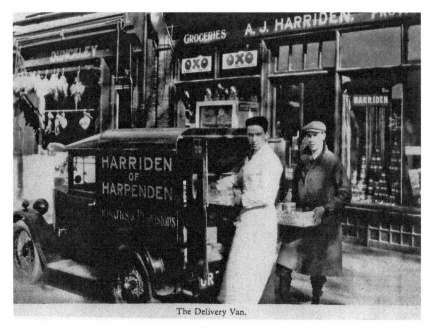

The Delivery Van.

Harriden's Grocery Store

Harriden's grocery store in Lower High Street in the 1930s. In one of the windows was a coffee roasting machine, which emitted a heady aroma of roasting beans. The smell was wonderful. Here the shop assistant is helping the driver to load the van ready for his daily delivery to their customers in the village. Harriden's finally closed its doors in the 1970s. Perry the florist now occupies the premises. Although around seventy years have elapsed between these two photos, the frontage had barely changed when the lower one was taken in 2006, still maintaining the distinctive double doors and decorative lattice work under the windows on either side of the entrance. Today, only the exterior paintwork colour has changed to this prestigious local shop.

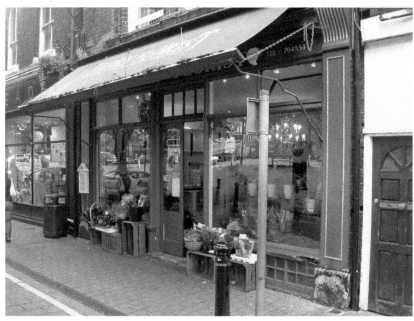

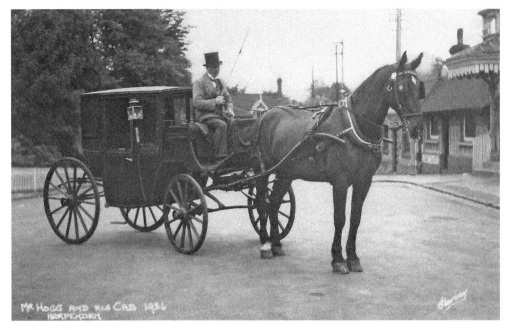

William Hogg

Although the age of the horse-drawn cab was sadly fast disappearing by the mid-1930s, William Hogg and his cab, seen above waiting for a fare outside Harpenden station, was still popular for many evening commuters who often favoured this mode of transport to the motorised taxis. William continued working until his death aged sixty-five in 1936. In his younger days, he caused quite a stir in 1891 when he drove his horse into the Cock Pond to cool off, only for the poor animal to get stuck in the mud. Soon helping hands had managed to get the animal back on dry land again, presumably none the worse for the experience as can be seen below, although within a few hours the whole village knew about the unfortunate incident.

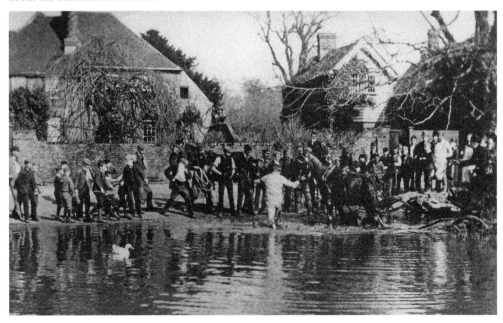

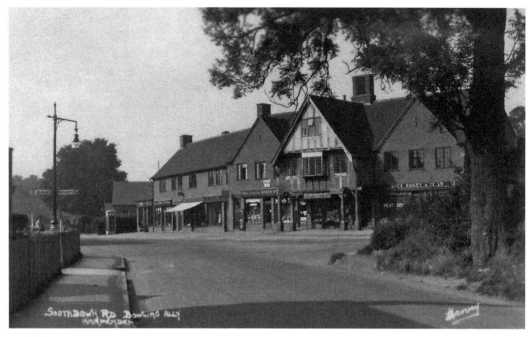

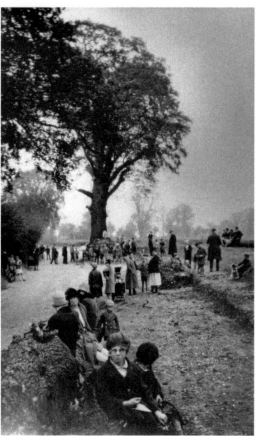

Southdown

A short distance from the centre of Harpenden lies the lovely suburb of Southdown. With the continuing growth of this area, and in order to accommodate the steady increase in motorised traffic, a decision was made by the Urban District Council to fell a large tree in Piggottshill Lane, just seen to the right of the picture, so that the road could be widened. Tuesday 20 May 1930 was the day that workmen arrived to carry out the job, and with the local photographer in attendance and a small crowd of curious onlookers gathered to witness the event, the task was soon accomplished.

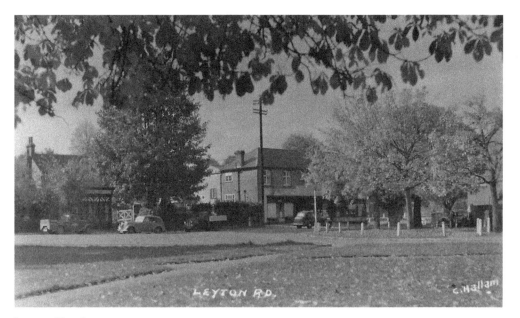

Leyton Road

This tranquil setting of Leyton Road on a lovely summer's day shows the popular Mary-Ellen's tearooms on the left of the photo, which opened in the early 1930s. Prior to this, the property belonged to Henry Salisbury who had started his business, Salisbury's Cycle Depot, in the 1880s. Henry not only sold bicycles, but was also an ironmonger as well.

Further along Leyton Road is an attractive open space called Leyton Green, as depicted below. It was here in 1939, just before the outbreak of the Second World War, that two air-raid shelters were constructed below ground, each with a capacity for around 100 people. On 14 May 1913, Harpenden's first cinema, the White Palace, opened for business. It occupied a position on the corner of Amenbury Lane, just out of camera shot, at the junction with Leyton Road, closing in 1933 when the nearby Regent Cinema opened.

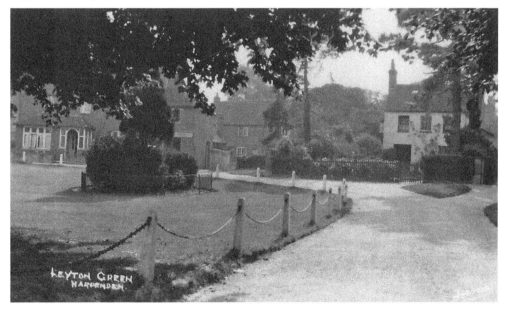

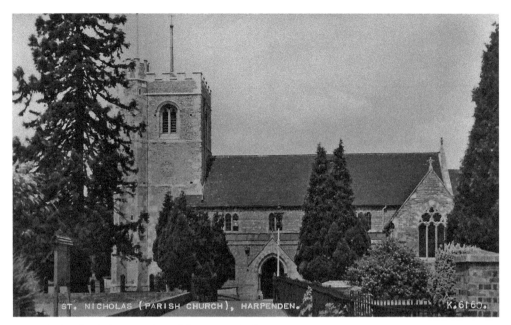

St Nicholas Parish Church and Batchelor's Row

The above picture shows St Nicholas Parish Church, the oldest church in Harpenden, originally built in the thirteenth-century. Although most of the old church was demolished in the early 1860s to be replaced by a larger building, the tower dates back to 1470 and contains a ring of eight bells, the oldest of which is dated from 1612. The new church was consecrated on 7 November 1862 with Canon Vaughan as Harpenden's first rector.

The attractive wintry scene below depicts a row of sixteenth-century cottages called Batchelor's Row that front Church Green. These were, at one time or another during the 1920s and 1930s, occupied by the surgery of Doctors Maclean, Fraser and Ross; Miss Morgan, the headmistress of the nearby Church Infant School; and George William Curl, the parish clerk and sexton. Despite much local opposition, the cottages were demolished in the late 1950s to make way for a parade of shops and Harpenden's first supermarket.

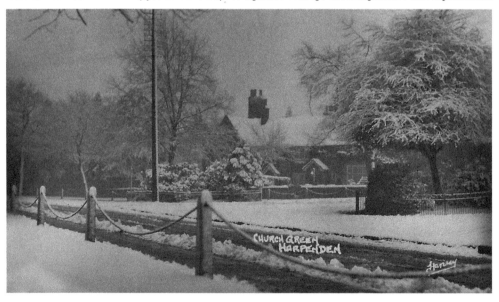

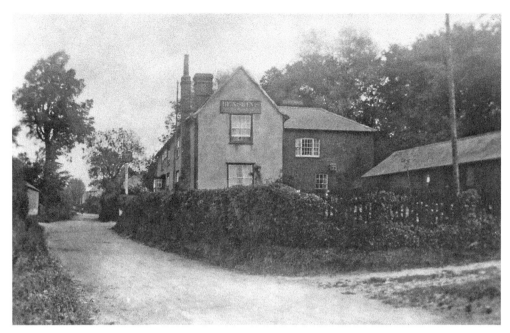

The Marquis of Granby

During the 1930s, mine host of this quaint eighteenth-century Grade II-listed old inn situated at the bottom of Crabtree Lane, the Marquis of Granby, was one Alfred Edward Mundy. He was known as Alf to his many regulars, some who are seen below enjoying a sociable drink in the pub's beer garden. Although fully licensed, Alf also provided teas and ices, which were always welcome on a hot summer's day. Being so close to the adjacent River Lea and ford, where horses and wagons once crossed with their heavy loads, the old pub used to have a clear view of the riverside scenery, but over the intervening years tall trees, shrubs and vegetation have gradually obstructed the outlook. Originally called the Swan, the inn became the Marquis of Granby in 1799.

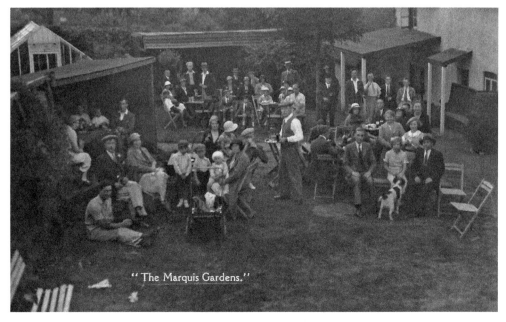

"The Marquis Gardens."

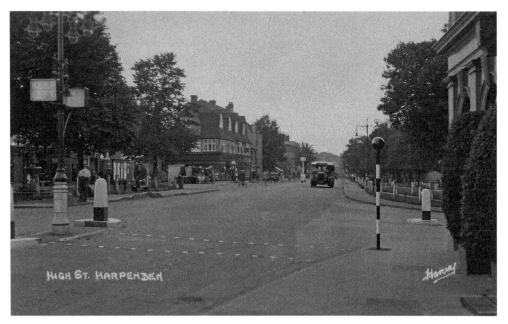

Junction of High Street and Station Road

The High Street in the mid-1930s at the junction with Station Road. This delightful picture shows the new Belisha beacon pedestrian crossing outside the Railway Hotel (now the Harpenden Arms). The beacon, so named after the then Minister of Transport Leslie Hore-Belisha, was introduced in 1934 and consisted of a round orange lamp on top of a black and white pole. The image also captures a way of life long since disappeared, from the ornate gas lamp standards to the lovely old single-decker bus and Austin 7 where, without the encumbrance of yellow lines and other restrictions, the motorist could park anywhere in the village without incurring a penalty fine. The image below was taken on the other side of the road opposite the Railway Hotel.

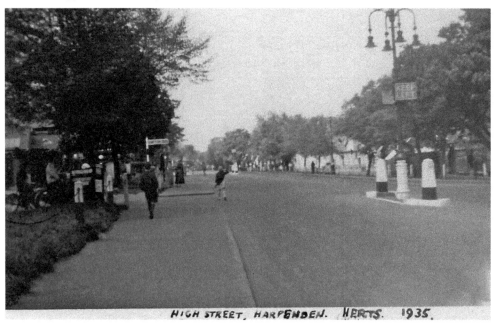

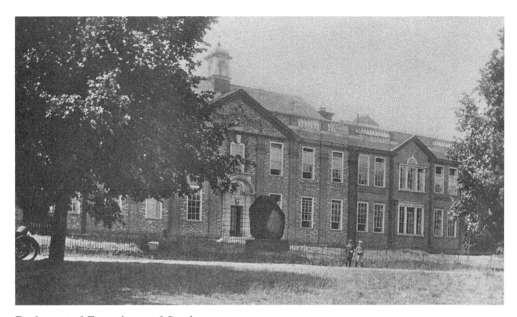

Rothamsted Experimental Station

John Bennet Lawes, who founded Rothamsted Experimental Station in 1843, was born at Rothamsted Manor on 28 December 1814. As a young man he became interested in the effects of fertilisers on crop growth and in 1843, together with Dr Joseph Gilbert, started a series of field experiments to develop and establish the principles of crop nutrition. The Russell Building above was a purpose-made laboratory constructed in 1917 to replace the old Testimonial Building that had been built in 1855 by public subscription of farmers nationwide in appreciation of the benefits their experiments were bringing to agriculture. Prominently featured centrally is the Shap granite monument that was erected in 1893 to commemorate fifty years of research. Just out of view in the charming photographic image of Hatching Green below, a small hamlet a short distance from Harpenden, is Manor Drive, once the main entrance to Rothamsted Manor.

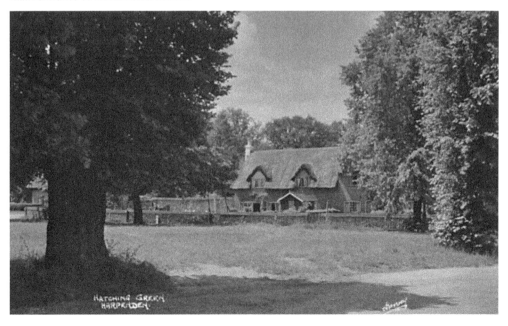

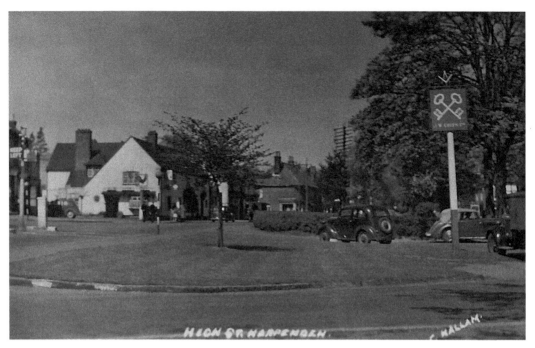

The Old Cock Inn

Two lovely postcards of differing seasons depicting the Old Cock Inn – both were taken from outside the Cross Keys public house across the road. Interestingly, two of the nineteenth-century landlords of the Cock both had additional occupations. Around 1851, Joseph Trustram, who was also a carpenter, used to hire out threshing tackle with a team of six horses to local farmers, while the landlord in the 1890s was listed as a wheelwright. Both photos were taken by the prolific local photographer Cecil Hallam.

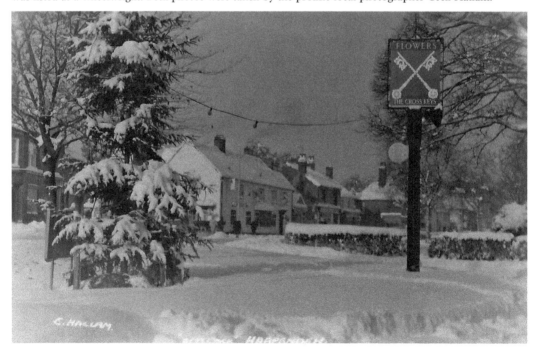

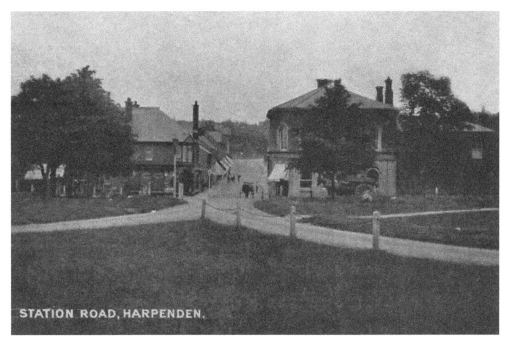

Station Road

Two delightful photographs capturing the view when looking towards Station Road during the 1930s, a time when the development of the village was rapidly growing. In both pictures Ridley's the ironmongers was still trading, although closure would come in 1933 when the Midland Bank took over the premises. On the opposite corner is the Railway Hotel, which was built in 1871, three years after the coming of the railway in 1868. In the early days there were livery stables attached to the hotel where horses could be hired for the local hunt meet.

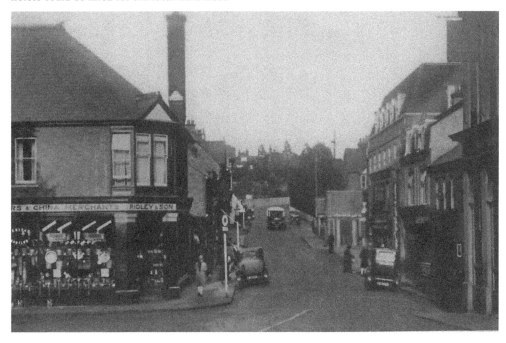

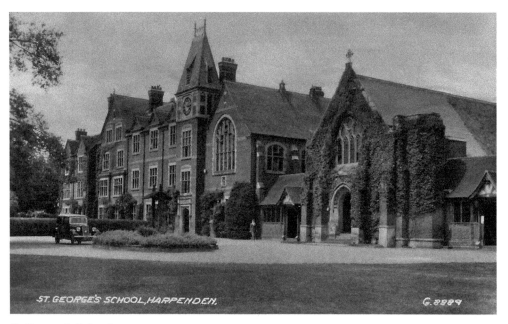

St George's School

The above image, showing the purpose-built school that would be St George's, was posted on 5 August 1939, less than one month before the start of the Second World War. It was started in 1885, with possession taken at the end of January 1887 under the headmastership of Robert Henry Wix, a scholar of Peterhouse, Cambridge, who had been head of a school, also called St George's, in Brampton, Huntingdon. Following Mr Wix's retirement in 1904 the school buildings were leased to the United Services College, who were only in residence until 1906. The following year the present school was founded by Revd Cecil Grant, who, with his wife Lucy, had until recently been running a co-educational school in Keswick based on firm Christian family principles. The chapel was built in 1891.

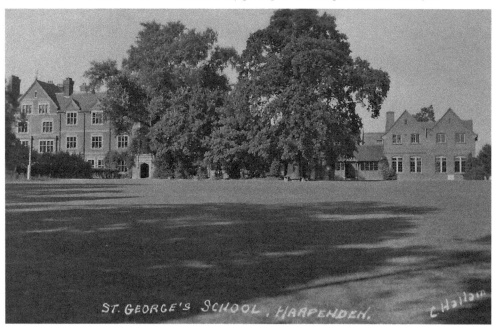

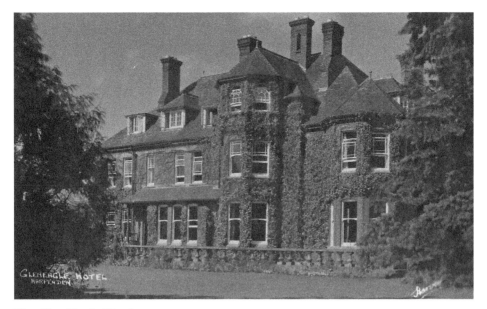

The Glen Eagle Hotel

At the northern end of the village, where the High Street becomes Luton Road, and situated on opposing corners of Townsend Lane were the Kirkwick Hotel and Car Trailers Ltd. The hotel was originally a large nineteenth-century house built in the 1880s for Captain Charles Braithwaite who held several key positions in Harpenden Conservative Club. By 1928 it had become the Kirkwick Hotel, described in an advertisement of the time as a 'charming house standing on gravel soil in 2 ½ acres of grounds'. A further change of ownership took place in 1939 when it was renamed the Glen Eagle Hotel, and by 2008 it was the Glen Eagle Manor Hotel. Today, after extensive alterations, the building is now called Gleneagle Manor, a large complex of luxury apartments. As can be seen in the 1930s advertising postcard below, Car Trailers Ltd offered a tent trailer with either one or two lean-tos that could easily be erected, a brilliant concept that would appear to have been way ahead of its time.

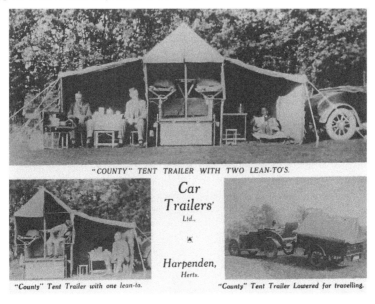

"COUNTY" TENT TRAILER WITH TWO LEAN-TO'S.

Car Trailers' Ltd..

Harpenden, Herts.

"County" Tent Trailer with one lean-to.   "County" Tent Trailer Lowered for travelling.

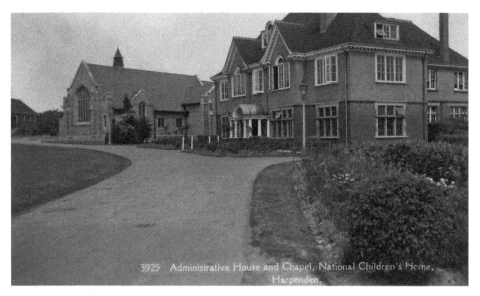

3925 Administrative House and Chapel, National Children's Home, Harpenden.

The National Children's Home and Sanatorium

The National Children's Home was founded by Dr Thomas Bowman Stephenson in 1869, initially in a small cottage near Waterloo Station in London, before moving to larger accommodation in Bonner Road, Bethnal Green, two years later. In 1913, the home transferred to a 300-acre site in Ambrose Lane, Harpenden, where a large central grass oval separated the girls' houses to the left of the entrance and the boys' to the right. Upon reaching school-leaving age, a variety of trades were taught and apprenticeships offered to the boys in the on-site Printing School. Girls were trained in various secretarial duties, such as shorthand and typewriting, or as seamstresses.

The delightful building below, with its distinctive veranda overlooking the beautiful gardens, was purpose-built in 1910 as a sanatorium, part of the National Children's Home, for children at risk of or suffering from tuberculosis. Situated in the rambling countryside on the outskirts of north Harpenden a short distance from the orphanage, the young patients were often wheeled onto the veranda during the summer months as it was felt that the benefits of fresh air were deemed to aid recovery.

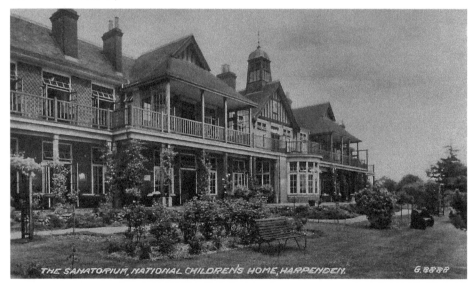

THE SANATORIUM, NATIONAL CHILDREN'S HOME, HARPENDEN.   G. 8888

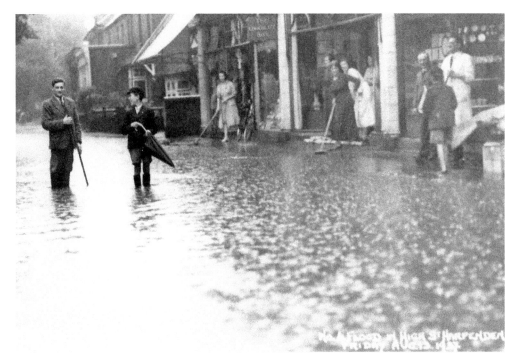

Flooding in Lower High Street

Following a downpour of heavy rain on 13 August 1937, these shopkeepers in Lower High Street arrived for work to find that their premises were waterlogged and the street flooded. Lower High Street had always been prone to flooding, as can be seen in the picture below, especially before the small stream that flowed from the Cock Pond was piped underground in 1928.

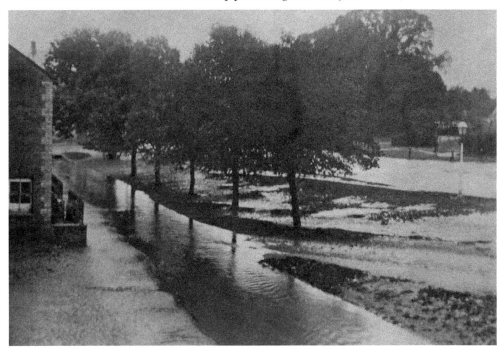

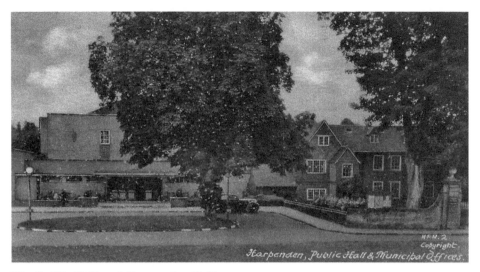

The Public Hall and Harpenden Hall

Since opening its doors in 1938, the Public Hall in Southdown Road has seen a variety of events, from the popular Saturday night dances to the eagerly awaited annual *Scout Gang Show*. Today, the building is known as the Harpenden Public Halls and divided into the Eric Morecambe Hall, named after the famous comedian who lived in the village from the early 1960s until his untimely death in 1984, and the smaller Southdown Room.

Just to the right of the Public Hall is Harpenden Hall. It was built in the sixteenth century, and over the years has seen many changes of occupancy over its long history, including at one time a private asylum and more recently the offices of the Urban District Council. From 1910 until 1923 it was a girls' boarding school catering for twenty pupils and run by a Miss English. For the next eight years, from 1924 until 1931, the hall was taken over by St Dominic's Convent School before they moved the short distance down Southdown Road to their new premises in the Welcombe, once the home of Henry Tylston Hodgson, a local benefactor and the deputy chairman of the Midland Railway.

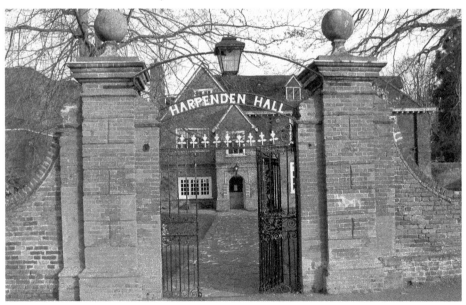

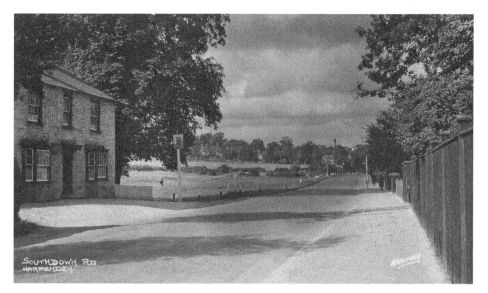

The Bowling Alley

Part of Southdown, also known as the Bowling Alley, is shown above in this real photograph card taken in the 1920s/1930s, with the Queen's Head public house on the left and the Common in the distance. The origin of the name 'Bowling Alley', according to a local source, does not come from the game but from the shape of a field. In 1784 there were two fields, Upper and Lower Bowling Alley, which were later combined before Longfield Road was eventually built over them.

The iconic image below (taken from the opposite direction from the one above) shows Skew Bridge, described as 'an amazing marvel of engineering' at that time. It was constructed in 1865 for the Midland Railway line that was to pass through Harpenden, which opened in 1868 with two tracks. Skew Bridge was widened in 1891 and a further two tracks added. The old cottages on the right were demolished in the 1960s when the site was redeveloped with modern housing. The photographic postcard, which was taken by local photographer Oliver Harvey and posted on the 15 November 1937, was captured at just the right time as the London train passed over the bridge on its approach to Harpenden.

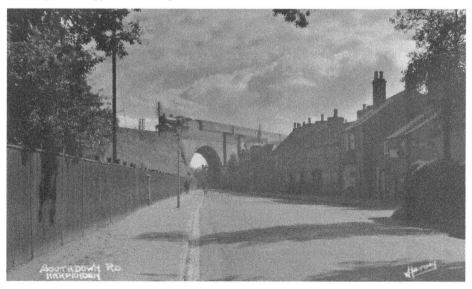

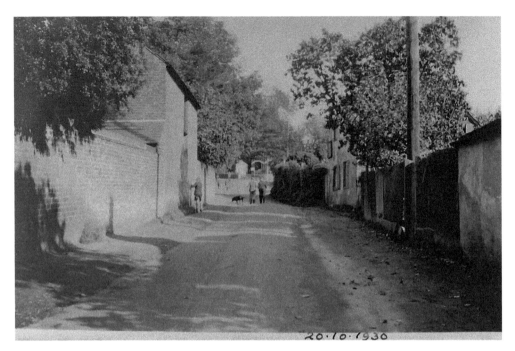

20·10·1930

Bowers Way

With Sun Lane featured in the above picture taken on 20 October 1930, the construction of Bowers Way below is an excellent photographic example of the development taking place in Harpenden during the interwar years of the 1920s and 1930s. Originally a cul-de-sac, Bowers Way, a turning on the right-hand side as you travelled up Sun Lane from the High Street, was built in the early 1930s at the same time that the lane was widened. The sign above the Estate Office offers 'Secluded & Distinctive Houses, Carefully & Tastefully Decorated', a claim that these were and still are highly desirable residences. Bowers Way was eventually linked with Victoria Road in the 1960s.

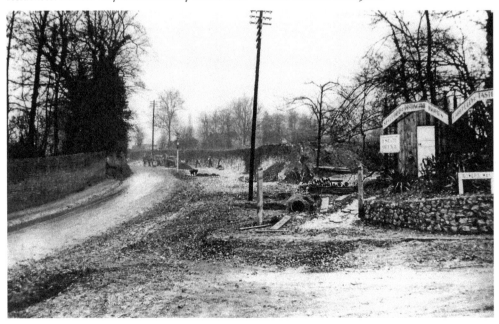

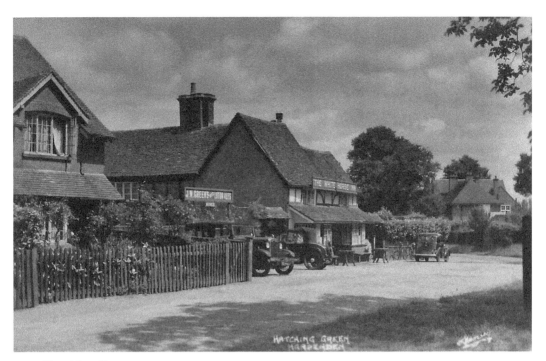

Hatching Green

These delightful 1930s images are of the seventeenth-century Grade II-listed White Horse public house, a popular venue situated on a quiet country lane on what is now the B487 to Redbourn in the small hamlet of Hatching Green, a five minute drive from the busy centre of Harpenden.

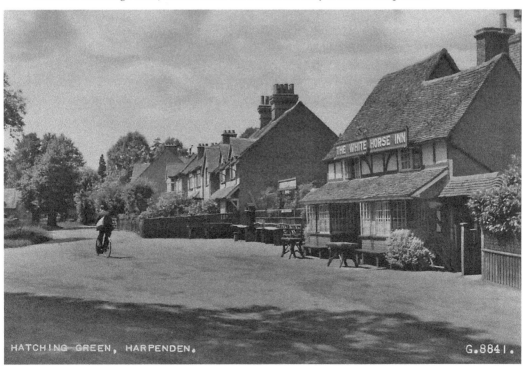

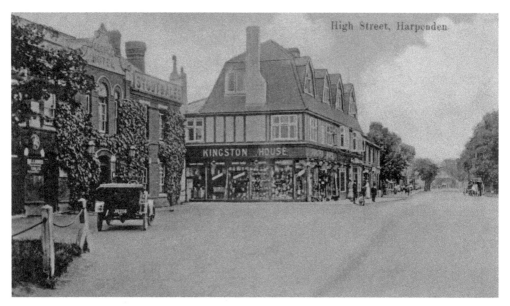

The George Hotel and Kingston House

This tranquil scene taken around 1920 shows the forecourt of the ivy-covered George Hotel, complete with a lovely old motor car, Kingston House store in the background and a High Street devoid of any traffic. A familiar sight in 1920 would have been that of fishmonger Mr Hammett, who travelled each day from Luton by horse and cart to sell his wares from a stall set up in front of The George. He later opened a shop in the High Street.

For nearly sixty years during the first half of the twentieth century one of the most flourishing businesses to trade in Harpenden was that of Kingston House, situated in the High Street next to The George Hotel. Built in 1912 by the firm originally started by Henry Salisbury, the store was constructed on the site of the then recently demolished house that had belonged to Dr Kingston, a local doctor. Selling a variety of household goods, Kingston House is probably best remembered for the sale and servicing of its extensive range of lawnmowers.

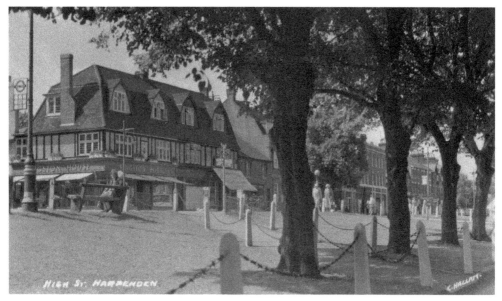

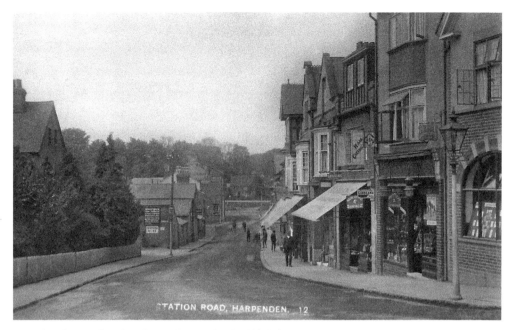

Looking Down Station Road Towards the High Street

Station Road as seen in 1927 from Station Approach looking towards the High Street. At the junction with Arden Grove on the left of the picture, part of the advertisement on the wall of the building states, 'Motor Landaulette Meets the Trains' with the telephone number given as '95' – no doubt the commuters of the day could avail themselves of a high-class taxi service. On the right-hand side a barber's shop displays the cost of a haircut at 4*d* and a shave at 2*d*, while next door above the premises of Charles Ernest Chirney, Cycle and Motor Agent, a small sign proclaims 'Humber Motor Cycles', indicating that these are readily available to purchase in the shop.

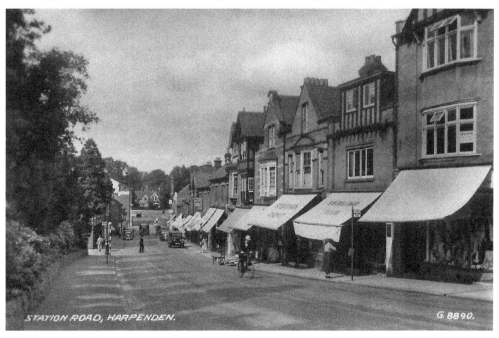

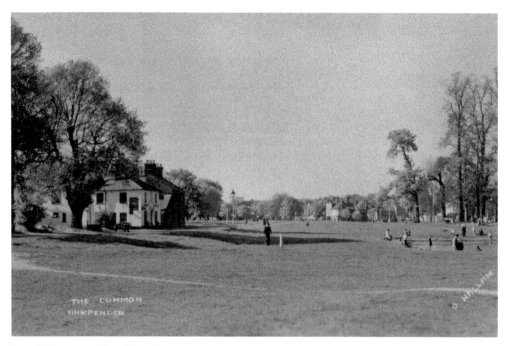

The Silver Cup Coaching Inn

One of the first introductions to the lovely town of Harpenden that the motorist will see as he travels from St Albans is depicted above. This idyllic view, taken on a sunny summer's day, shows the historic Silver Cup public house, a seventeenth-century coaching inn situated opposite the beautiful Harpenden Common a few hundred yards from the town, arguably one of the most attractive areas in the county, if not the country. Sadly the children's paddling pool on the right has long since gone due to being a potential health risk.

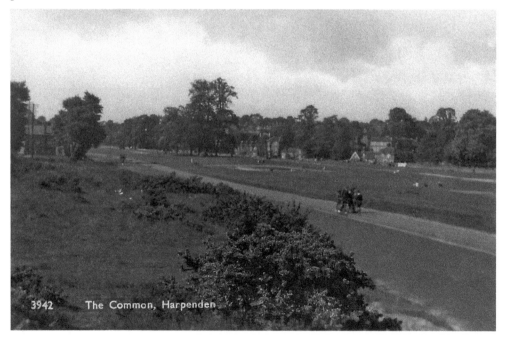

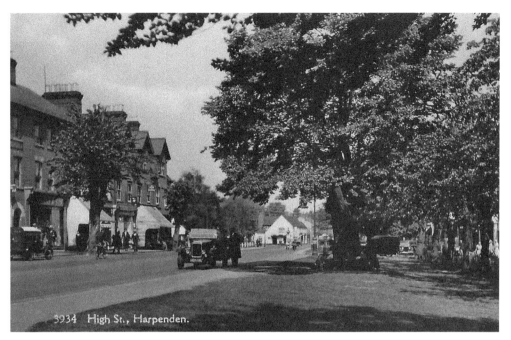

3934 High St., Harpenden.

Motoring in the 1930s

These were the days when petrol was cheap and motoring a real pleasure. The wide boulevard that is the High Street is vividly depicted in these two photos that were taken in the 1930s, where the peace and tranquillity of this lovely village is not yet marred by the traffic congestion and parking problems that were still over half a century away.

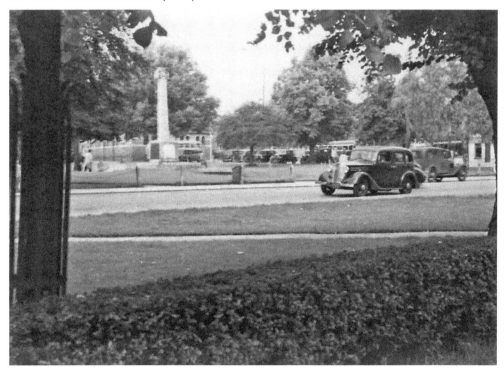

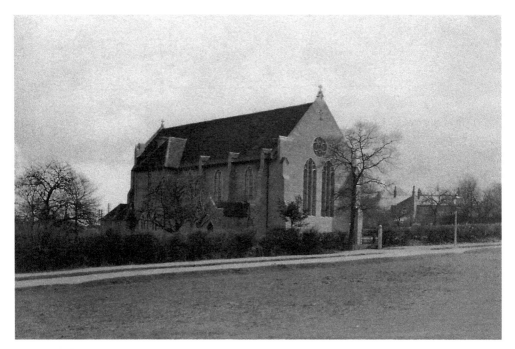

St John's Church

On the night of New Year's Eve 1905, the original St John's Church, known as the Paper Church because of its timber-frame construction, caught fire with the building being completely destroyed. The church had been erected in 1895 on the corner of what was then Wheathampstead Road, now Southdown Road, and Crabtree Lane. Following this devastating event a new church designed by Mr F. C. Eden, a noted architect, was built a short distance away in St John's Road. The new church was consecrated on 2 March 1908, with the Crabtree Lane site eventually being developed for housing.

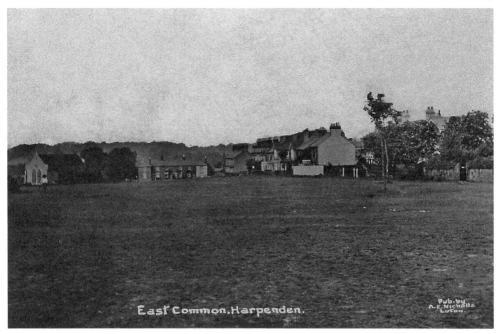

East Common, Harpenden.

Pub. by
A.E. Nicholls
Luton.

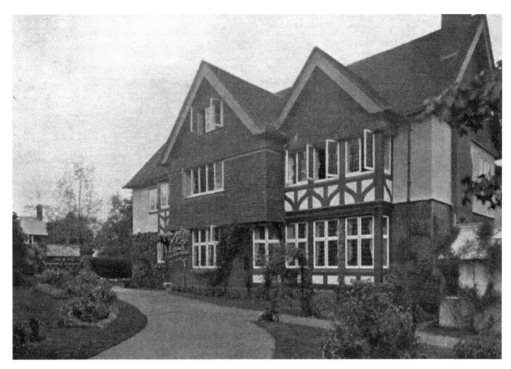

St Helena's College

Built in the late 1890s, St Helena's College was originally a small select school for young ladies, of which some were boarders. Sometime after the First World War the school closed and the building, which had been bought for £3,100 in 1920, became the Harpenden Memorial Nursing Centre in memory of those in the village who had given their lives in the conflict. The two pictures show the front and rear elevations of the college, which is now called St Helena's Court and is a tastefully converted block of flats.

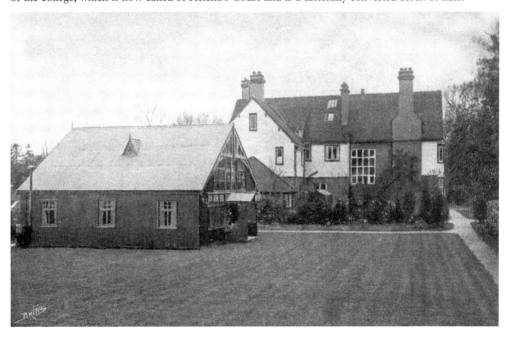

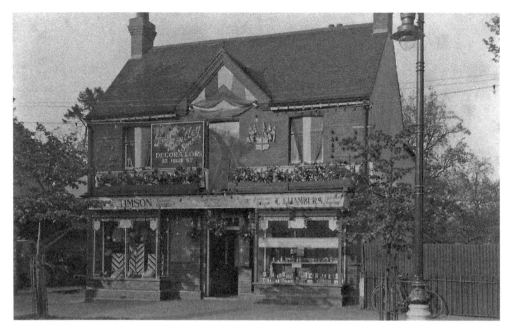

George V's Silver Jubilee

This picture was taken in 1935 at the time of George V's Silver Jubilee. Note the little glass nightlights picking out the letters 'G' and 'M' – George and Mary to the left and right of the top windows. The building was occupied by Fred Timson, an outfitter and bootmaker at No. 57; Tom Chambers, a hairdresser by profession who also used to repair umbrellas, had the shop next door at No. 57a; and on the first floor at No. 57b Frank Bentley carried out his decorating business.

The image below shows the High Street in the 1920s looking southwards, still showing the trees on the right-hand side of the road, which were not removed until 1935.

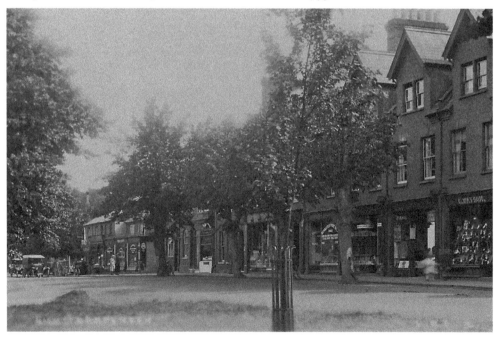

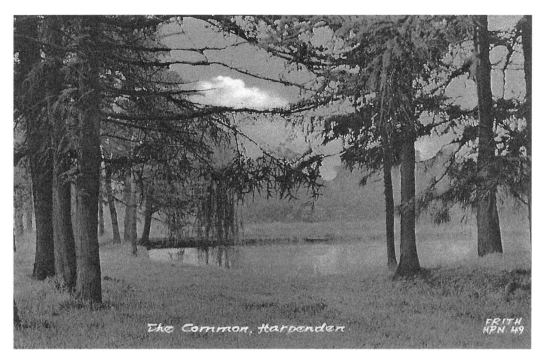

The Common, Harpenden

FRITH
HPN 49

'Little Switzerland'

These two lovely images of the ponds on the Common taken in the 1930s have truly captured their beauty, and rightly deserve the rather grand name of 'Little Switzerland' for this picturesque part of Harpenden.

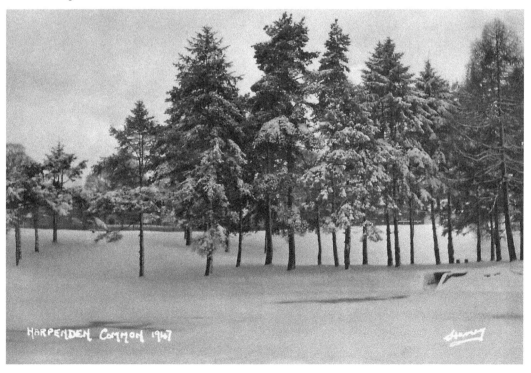

HARPENDEN Common 1947

Chapter 3

Storm Clouds of War Again

At precisely 11.15 a.m. on that fateful Sunday morning of 3 September 1939, like millions of people around the country, the residents of Harpenden were huddled around their wireless sets to hear the news that everyone expected but hoped would never happen: Prime Minister Neville Chamberlain broadcast to the nation that a state of war now existed between Britain and Germany.

Mr Chamberlain announced, 'This morning the British Ambassador in Berlin handed the German Government a final Note stating that, unless we heard from them by 11 o'clock that they were prepared at once to withdraw their troops from Poland, a state of war would exist between us.

I have to tell you now that no such undertaking has been received, and that consequently this country is at war with Germany.'

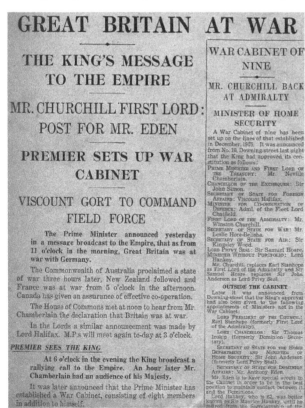

War declared.

Although the storm clouds of war had already started to gather as Germany, following the Anschluss of Austria in March 1938, marched into the Sudetenland, Czechoslovakia, on 1 October of the same year, once war had actually been declared by Great Britain and France on Nazi Germany, there was an eight-month period of virtual inactivity known as the Phoney War. This lasted until 10 May 1940 when Germany attacked France and the Low Countries.

However, during those months prior to that fateful September day, preparations had already started to be put in place in the event of invasion and aerial attack. These included digging trenches, the distribution of Anderson shelters, covering doors and windows to comply with blackout regulations, and sticking adhesive tape to the inside of windows as a protection in the event of a bomb blast, as well as the issue of gas masks

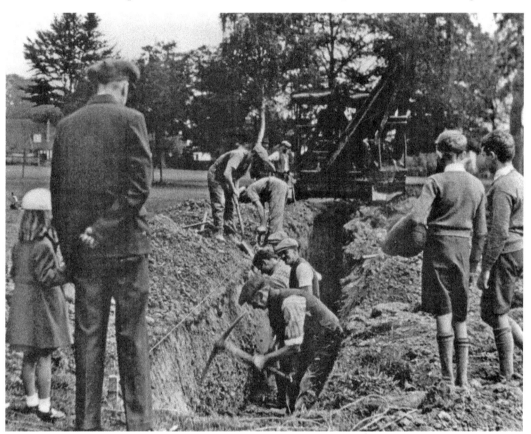

Preparing for Invasion
With the likelihood of war in that late summer of 1939, these young children are watching some workmen digging trenches. Memories of the 1914/18 conflict twenty years earlier are likely rekindled by the little girl's grandfather as preparations are made in Harpenden and all over the country for a possible enemy invasion.

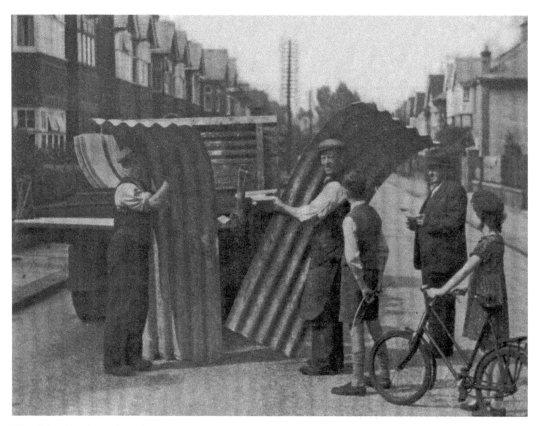

The Distribution of Anderson Air-Raid Shelters

Prior to the commencement of hostilities between Great Britain and Germany, and with aerial bombardment by the Luftwaffe a very real threat, all householders were issued with a free Anderson shelter as a means of protection. They were designed to accommodate up to six people and were named after the Home Secretary Sir John Anderson, the Lord Privy Seal and architect of Britain's policy on air-raid shelters.

The construction was based on a number of arched and straight galvanised corrugated-steel panels bolted together and sunk into a pit 3 or 4 feet deep in the householder's garden or backyard, with the roof covered in earth. When tested, this type of shelter performed well under blast and ground shock, and proved to be an exceptionally strong and effective solution when erected correctly. While the householder and his family might be relatively safe in an Anderson shelter, they were an extremely cold and uncomfortable way in which to spend the night, notwithstanding they were also very prone to dampness and flooding.

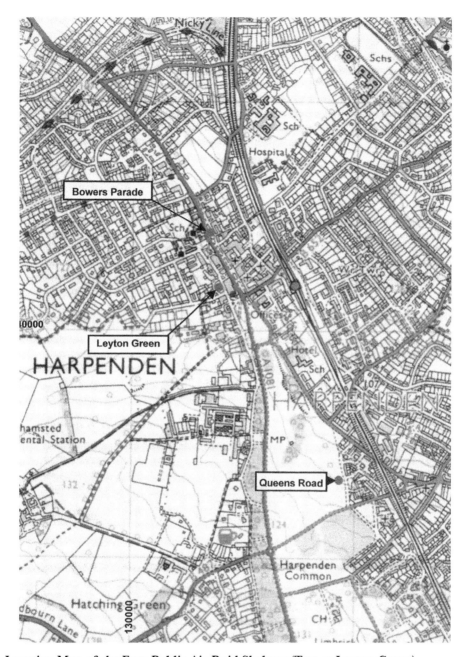

Location Map of the Four Public Air-Raid Shelters (Two at Leyton Green)
In addition to individual air-raid shelters there were also four large public shelters located in and around central Harpenden. The largest one, which was constructed in August 1939, was situated opposite Bowers Parade on the site of the village pond that had been drained and grassed over in 1928, and could accommodate 180 people.

It comprised 177 feet of passages in six sections with space for benches on both sides. There were stairways and toilets at each end with two escape hatches. Shelters could also be found at Leyton Green in Leyton Road where there were two with a capacity for 100 people in each, and at Queens Road in South Harpenden where there was one with a capacity for 120 people.

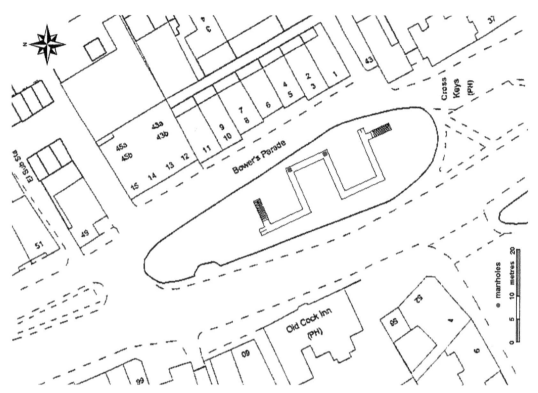

Plan of Bowers Parade Air-Raid Shelter.

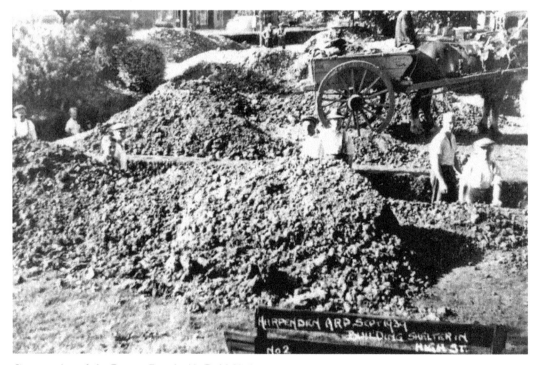

Construction of the Bowers Parade Air-Raid Shelter.

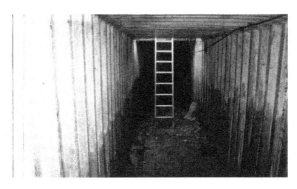

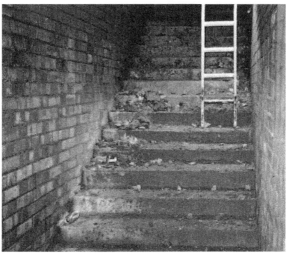

The Interior of Bowers Parade Air-Raid Shelter

After rejecting the offer of an Anderson shelter, one local resident decided to build his own means of protection by constructing a reinforced-concrete bunker in his back garden, which when compared to the Anderson was the epitome of 'luxury'. Sunk deep into the ground, the entrance was accessed through a pair of bomb-proof metal doors that revealed a flight of a dozen or so concrete steps leading downwards. At the bottom was another metal door, which opened into a domed chamber that was just big enough to stand up in and accommodated two double bunk beds on either side of a narrow walkway.

Sleeping conditions were apparently very cramped and the pungent oily smell from the hurricane lamp made the air stale and heavy. At the far end was a narrow shaft with metal rungs built into the brickwork. This led up to an escape hatch that could be used in the event that the occupants were unable to exit by the steps.

Two days before the declaration of war on 3 September 1939, night-time blackout regulations were imposed by the government. All windows and doors should be covered with a suitable material such as heavy curtains, cardboard or paint to prevent any glimmer of light escaping that might aid enemy aircraft. Vehicle headlights were fitted with slotted covers that enabled their beams to be deflected towards the ground. This, together with the lack of street lighting and dimmed traffic lights, caused thousands of people to die in road accidents. To help overcome this unnecessary loss of life, white stripes were painted on roads and on lamp posts.

To protect people from injury from the flying glass of broken windows during an air raid, each house was given some rolls of brown adhesive tape to stick to the inside of all windows from corner to corner in a diagonal pattern. This was to prevent shards of glass from flying into the rooms in the event of a bomb blast.

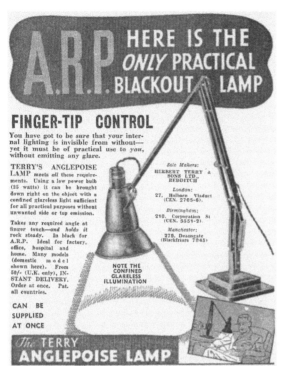

A.R.P HERE IS THE *ONLY* PRACTICAL BLACKOUT LAMP

FINGER-TIP CONTROL

You have got to be *sure* that your internal lighting is invisible from without—yet it must be of practical use to *you*, without emitting any glare.

TERRY'S ANGLEPOISE LAMP meets *all* these requirements. Using a low power bulb (25 watts) it can be brought down right on the object with a confined glareless light sufficient for all practical purposes without unwanted side or top emission.

Takes any required angle at finger touch—*and holds it* rock steady. In black for A.R.P. Ideal for factory, office, hospital and home. Many models (domestic model shown here). From 50/- (U.K. only), INSTANT DELIVERY. Order at once. Pat. all countries.

CAN BE SUPPLIED AT ONCE

Sole Makers:
HERBERT TERRY & SONS LTD.
REDDITCH

London:
27, Holborn Viaduct (CEN. 2705-6).

Birmingham:
210, Corporation St (CEN. 5551-2).

Manchester:
278, Deansgate (Blackfriars 7945)

NOTE THE CONFINED GLARELESS ILLUMINATION

The TERRY **ANGLEPOISE LAMP**

Air Raid Precaution Advert

With the blackout now in force, civilian Air Raid Precaution (ARP) wardens patrolled their allotted area to ensure that no house showed the slightest chink or glow of light, with offenders liable to stringent legal penalties. Very often the strident voice of the warden could be heard shouting 'PUT THAT LIGHT OUT' to one of the residents who had unfortunately incurred a brief lapse in the regulations.

The Civil Defence Service was a civilian volunteer organisation established in 1935 by the Home Office. In 1941, the use of civil defence replaced the pre-existing air raid precautions, although this was still included, together with wardens, firemen (initially the Auxiliary Fire Service (AFS) and latterly the National Fire Service (NFS)), fire watchers, rescue, first-aid posts and stretcher parties.

Over 1.9 million people served in civil defence and nearly 2,400 lost their lives to enemy action. The service was disbanded on 2 May 1945.

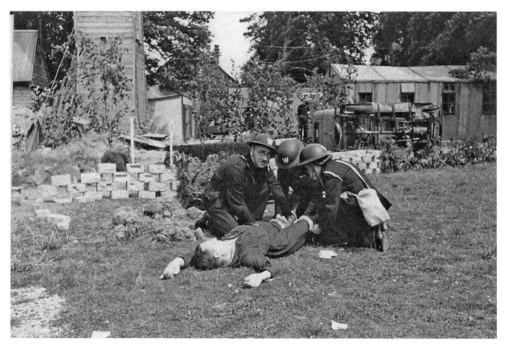

Civil Defence Wardens Competing in an Exercise

The photograph above shows a team of civil defence wardens competing in an exercise to test their abilities in being able to deal with 'bombing casualties' at the rear of Park Hall, Leyton Road, in August 1942.

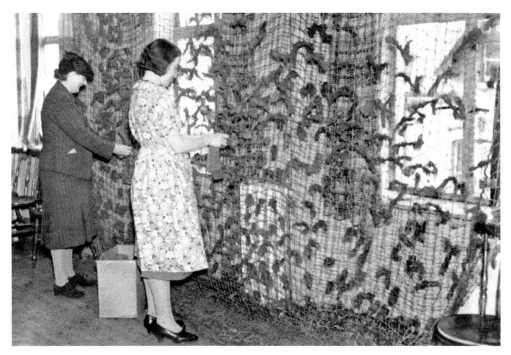

British Legion Volunteers Making Camouflage Netting

Once war was declared on Sunday 3 September 1939 the Government Evacuation Scheme was implemented. Almost 1.5 million civilians – mostly children – were evacuated from British cities to relative safety in the country. Harpenden was no exception and received some 1,500 children from London, many from the East End, either being housed (or billeted, as it was called) with local families or at the Evacuee Hostel in Hollybush Lane and a medical centre at Bowers Parade in the centre of Harpenden.

This was an extremely traumatic time for everyone; not only for the householder, but also for the young evacuee(s) who were being billeted with complete strangers, entering into what could be an unknown period of time spent apart from their families.

Like everyone else, all children were issued with a gas mask. Each contained in its own small brown cardboard box suspended from a string lanyard, and had to be carried at all times. There was also a special 'Mickey Mouse' version for young children.

By September 1939 some 38 million masks had been distributed as a protection against gas bombs that could be dropped during an air-raid, a fear generated by the amount of gas used during the First World War. The masks were never actually used though as no gas attack was ever used against the British.

It was during the war that Vauxhall Motors, situated just 6 miles from Harpenden, turned over its production from the manufacture of motor cars to that of Bedford lorries, and later in 1941 to the new Churchill Mark IV (A22) tanks, of which approximately 5,640 were built by 1945.

In order for the tanks and lorries to be put through their paces, the grounds of the nearby Luton Hoo estate, owned by the Wernher family, were used as a testing site. Later models were road tested, travelling on a circular route up Cutenhoe Road, Luton, along Luton Road towards Harpenden and returning to the Vauxhall plant via Thrales End Lane and the Lower Luton Road.

Occasionally the tank crew would stop at Green Lawns (once a fashionable country club but now a petrol station and restaurant on the A6 at Kinsbourne Green) halfway between Luton and Harpenden, where they would enjoy a welcome cup of tea. For many years after the war the impressions made by the tanks' tracks as they travelled along Thrales End Lane were still visible in the tarmac.

Following the German invasion of Soviet Russia on 22 June 1941 under the code name of 'Operation Barbarossa' the Russians were now an ally of Britain. As such, Soviet Trade Delegations, which included experts in tank engineering, would often visit the Vauxhall site and Luton Hoo.

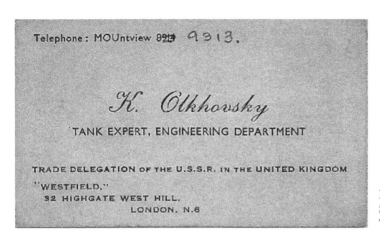

Business card of a Soviet Trade Delegation Tank expert.

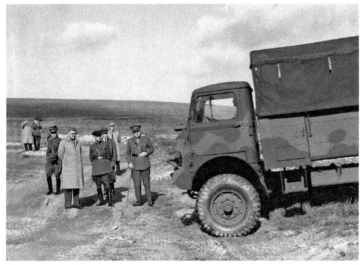

A Bedford Truck being shown to a visiting Soviet Trade Delegation at the Luton Hoo test site.

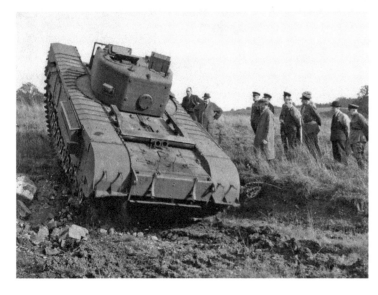

A Churchill Tank on test at Luton Hoo.

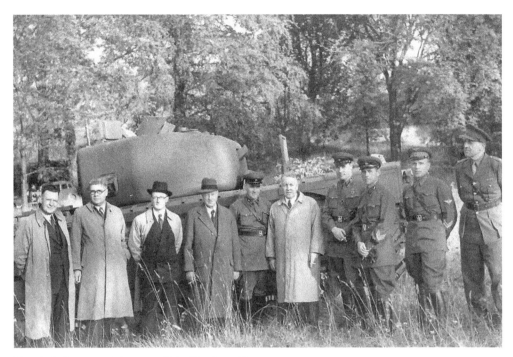

Vauxhall directors with some of the Russian visitors.

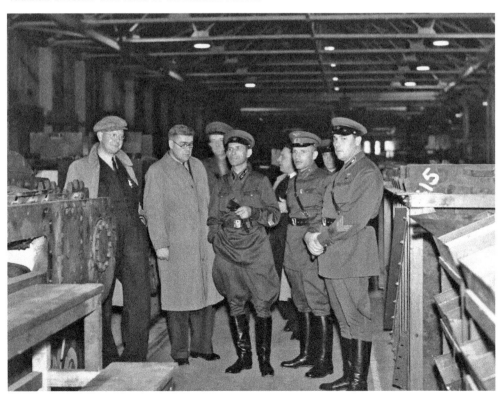

A Soviet Trade Delegation on a factory tour of the Vauxhall site.

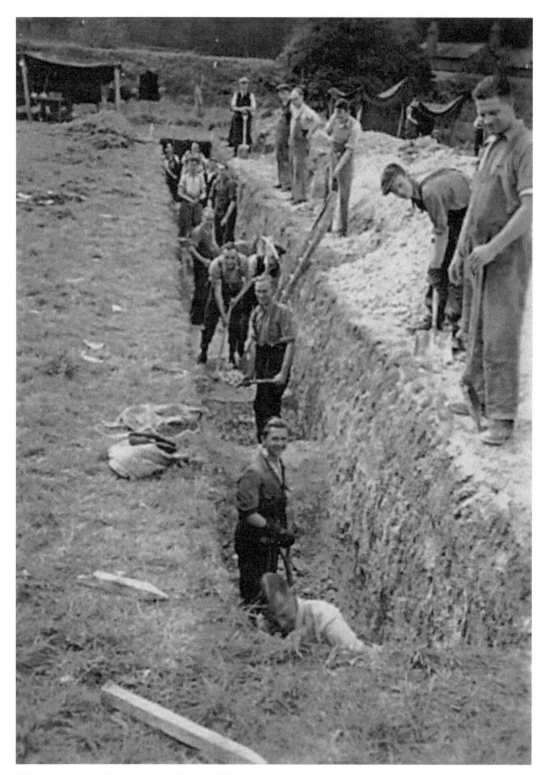

Digging an air-raid trench on the Vauxhall Motors site.

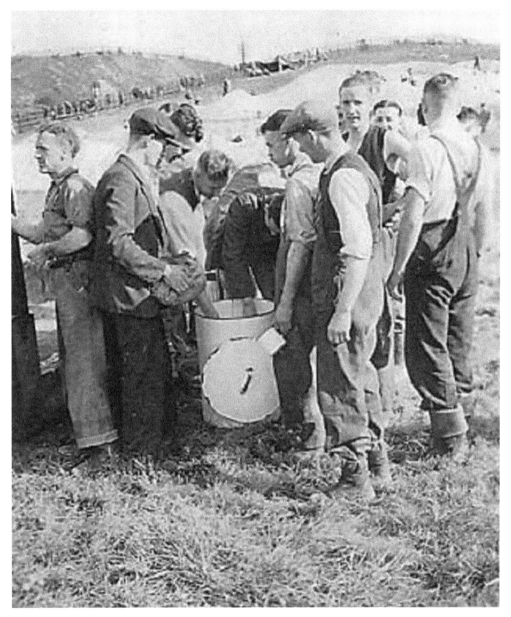

A 'Nice Cuppa Tea' Makes a Welcome Break from Digging Trenches

Vauxhall Motors, together with other key industries in the Luton area, were all prone to enemy bombardment due to their invaluable contribution to the war effort. Yet, most of the attacks appeared to be random rather than the saturation raids that the authorities expected, similar to the fate suffered by Coventry.

It was on the night of 10/11 May 1941 that the grim news bulletins on the wireless recounted the utter devastation in London, where they had just experienced the worst raid of the Blitz. Over 500 enemy bombers had dropped their deadly loads, killing in excess of 1,400 people and injuring hundreds more.

Night after night, from September 1940 until May 1941, German bombers had dropped their deadly cargo on not only London but on other British cities, ports and industrial areas as well. Viewed from as far away as Harpenden, the night sky over the capital could be seen as constantly tinged with orange as London burned, causing both death and destruction.

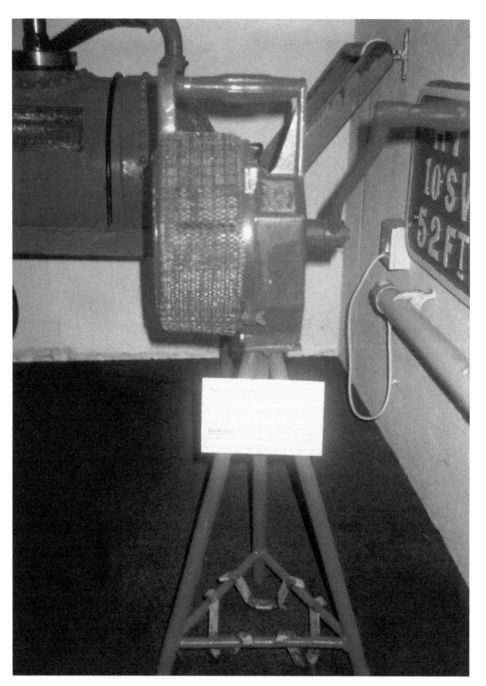

A Manual Air-Raid Siren

With the war now into its second year, the nocturnal visits to the air-raid shelters, coupled with rationing and severe shortages, formed a regular uninterrupted pattern in people's daily lives. The sounds of the sirens rising and falling in a crescendo put fear and dread into your whole body. You then left the comfort of your bed and hurried into the cold night air to the shelter in the garden or backyard, the deep throb of the turbo engines from the bombers passing overhead and then eventually the relief of the 'all clear'. These images are all indelibly etched on one's memory.

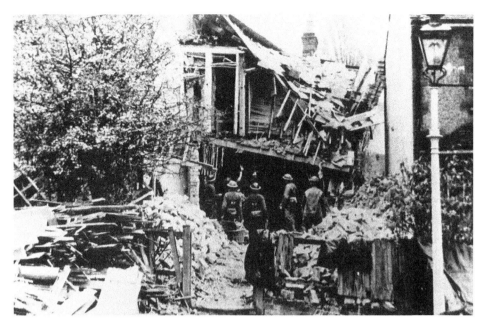

No. 10 Crabtree Lane just after being bombed.

Down — But Rising Again

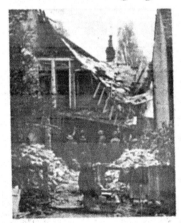

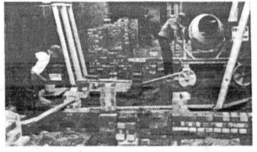

HARPENDEN'S BOMB DAMAGE.—The only house in Harpenden to be destroyed by the Hun is now being re-constructed at 10, Crabtree-lane, as can be seen from the picture above. Struck by a high explosive bomb on a Sunday night in 1940, the occupants of the house—a mother and child—sheltered under the stairs and escaped injury, although badly shocked. The picture on the left, was taken on the morning after.

The News Report Showing the Bombing and Rebuilding of No. 10 Crabtree Lane
While London and other major cities sustained heavy and frequent bombing attacks night after night by German bombers causing utter devastation, Harpenden in contrast suffered comparatively lightly. Although some bombs did fall in the Harpenden area there was no loss of life or serious damage, apart from one house – No. 10 Crabtree Lane in the Southdown area – which was badly hit on the night of 20 October 1940. The occupants, the mother and her young son, survived the impact and escaped serious injury after having taken refuge under the stairs.

A total of 180 houses also sustained minor damage. Almost seven months later, on 12 May 1941, the roof of Batford Methodist Church was completely burnt out after a number of incendiary bombs had been dropped, but fortunately there were no casualties.

A few facts and figures for Harpenden

High Explosive Bombs	41
Oil Incendiary Bombs	1
Incendiary Bombs	2,099
Phosphorus Bombs	10
Crashed Aircraft (British)	1
	————
Alerts	941
	————
Houses Damaged	180

One morning, local residents discovered that the area in which they lived was completely littered with silver strips of aluminium foil. Passing Wellington or Lancaster bombers had dropped bundles of this foil, a practice code-named 'Window'. It was apparently used by the RAF to cause maximum interference to German radar and had started in 1943.

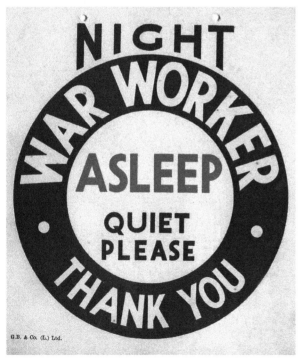

Quiet please!

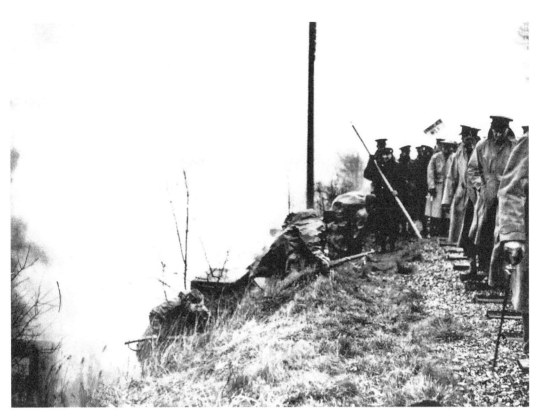

Manoeuvres in North Harpenden

With invasion now a real threat, an announcement was made on 14 May 1940 calling for all men between the ages of seventeen and sixty-five to enrol in a new force to act as Britain's 'last line of defence'. They were to be called the Local Defence Volunteers. By July, nearly 1.5 million men had enrolled and the name now changed to the Home Guard in accordance with a directive from Winston Churchill, who had assumed the position of prime minister in May.

Occasionally, the Harpenden force would carry out manoeuvres in the north part of the village. One such occurrence took place over a cold November weekend in 1942 when the Luton Road Bridge, known locally as The Arch, a short distance from Bloomfield Road, became a hive of activity as a combined exercise was carried out involving the local Home Guard and Civil Defence Service.

Watched by a team of military observers, a sustained attack was made on the bridge by the Home Guard, while low-flying aircraft from a United States Air Force base added a touch of realism to the proceedings.

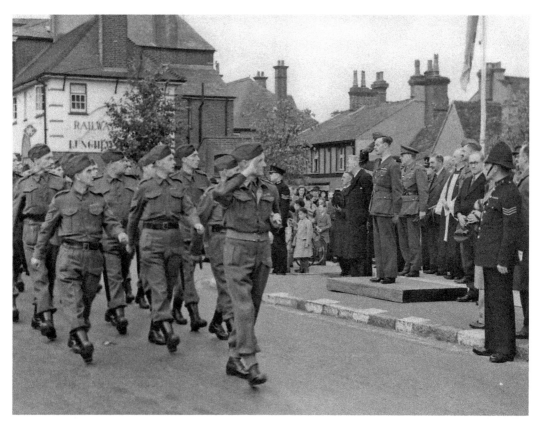

Wing Commander 'Bunny' Currant Taking the Salute at a Home Guard 'Wings for Victory Week' Parade Outside the Railway Hotel

During the Second World War, Harpenden Home Guard took part in several morale-boosting parades through the village, including 'War Savings Promotion Week' and a 'Wings for Victory Week' march. During the latter the salute was taken by one of the war's most successful fighter pilot aces, Wing Commander Christopher Frederick 'Bunny' Currant, DSO, DFC and Bar and the Croix de Guerre, a local man who was born in Luton. After leaving the RAF in 1959, Bunny joined Hunting Engineering in Luton, where he remained until his retirement in 1974.

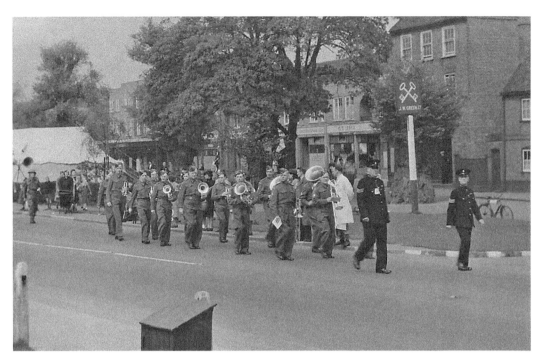

A 'War Savings Promotion Week' procession in April 1944 passing the Cross Keys public house in the High Street.

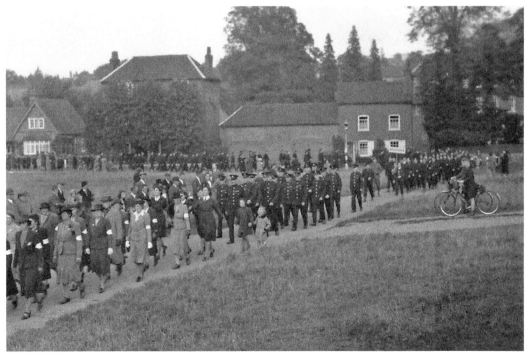

A procession of local organisations on Harpenden Common to mark 'Battle of Britain Sunday' on 26 September 1943.

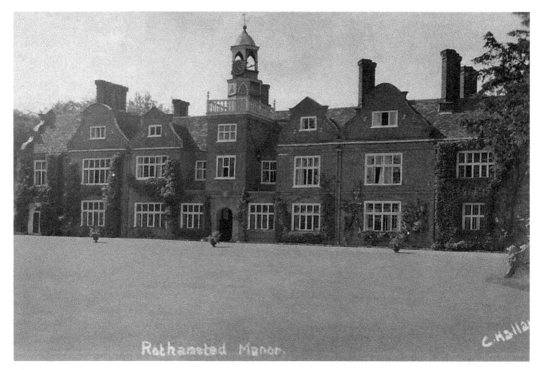

Rothamsted Manor.

Rothamsted Manor

One of the most clandestine activities to take place in wartime Harpenden was that which occurred at Rothamsted Manor, once the home of John Bennet Lawes, the founder of Rothamsted Experimental Station. It was here, as a top secret army intelligence centre, that 400 personnel were involved on the daily interceptions of Morse code radio messages between German Luftwaffe ground stations and airfields.

Once the information had been recorded, this was then forwarded by the quickest possible means to Bletchley Park in Buckinghamshire, the central site for British codebreakers. Teams of specialists that included mathematicians, crossword compilers, linguists and electronics experts would then process the data.

It was one of these brilliant mathematicians, Alan Turing, who was able to crack the 'Enigma' code, unbeknown to the enemy – the 'Enigma' being a type of enciphering machine used by the German armed forces to send messages securely.

Not knowing the true nature of what was taking place at Rothamsted Manor, there was certainly cause for much speculation among the locals as armed sentries patrolled the area and despatch riders were seen coming and going day and night. Thirty powerful radio receivers were manned twenty-four hours a day by specially trained operators who were drafted in from all over the country.

Following D-Day on 6 June 1944, operations changed from the Luftwaffe to German Army communications. Today the manor house forms an integral part of Rothamsted Research and is used as accommodation for the many visiting overseas scientists and for students who are trained on the site.

The Dam Busters

Unrelated to the war years in Harpenden but nevertheless worthy of a mention were the initial preparations for Operation Chastise, more commonly known as the Dambusters Raid. This took place a mere 12 miles from the village at the then Building Research Station (BRS) in Bricket Wood near St Albans. It was on the night of 16–17 May 1943 that nineteen modified Lancaster bombers of No. 617 Squadron, RAF Bomber Command, led by Wing Commander Guy Gibson, attacked the German Mohne, Eder and Sorpe dams in the heart of the industrial Ruhr using the famous bouncing bomb designed by Barnes Wallis of Vickers Armstrong.

In late 1940 a decision was made to construct a 1:50 scale model of the Mohne dam in a remote wooded part of the BRS site in order to resolve the problem of where to hit the dam and how much explosive to use. The undertaking was carried out in the utmost secrecy and involved the manufacture of over 2 million miniature mortar blocks, which were used to build a dam 42 feet long and nearly 3 feet high across a small stream. This was widened and deepened to provide a lake of the correct depth behind the dam.

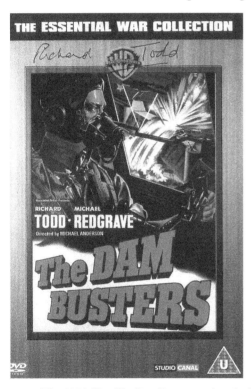 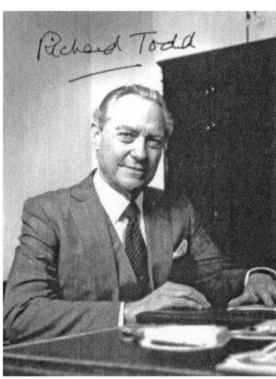

The 1954 film *The Dam Busters* starring the late Richard Todd, OBE.

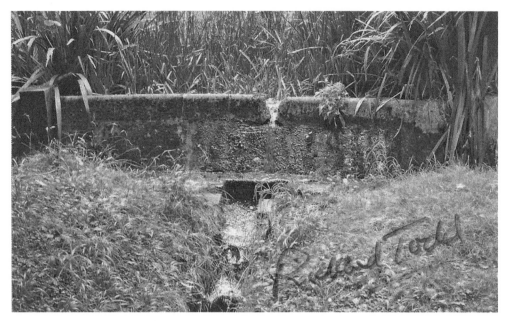

The Model of the Mohne Dam at the Building Research Establishment
Working long hours, often in sub-zero conditions, a small team of four completed the model in just seven weeks at a cost of £34 13s 9d in materials and labour. A series of explosive tests were then carried out during early 1941 by engineers from the Road Research Laboratory, which at that time was based at Harmondsworth, near West Drayton, Middlesex. After a number of tests, Wallis concluded that a charge of around 7,720 lbs exploded at a depth of 9 metres would be effective.

Although the project occupied the BRS staff for only a few short months in 1940 and 1941, it formed the basis for a further extensive programme of tests at the Road Research Laboratory, which culminated in the Mohne and Eder dams being breached causing catastrophic flooding of the Ruhr Valley and of villages in the Eder Valley. The Sorpe dam sustained only minor damage.

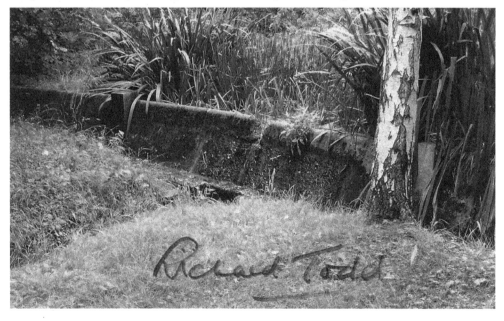

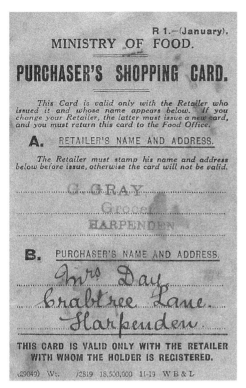

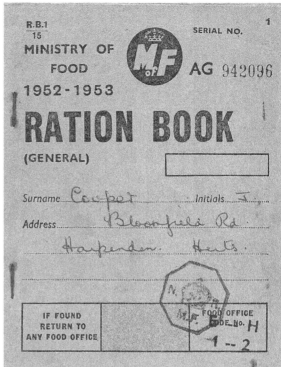

Rationing

Rationing started in 1940 and was to continue for a further fourteen years, although there was a gradual derationing of some basics starting with bread and jam, which came off in 1948. This was followed by tea in 1952; sugar, cream, eggs and sweets in 1953; and butter, meat and cheese in 1954.

Everyone had their own ration book but this entitlement to certain amounts of food or clothing did not necessarily mean that you were able to get them. It largely depended upon what the shopkeeper had available or, if you knew him well, what could be produced from 'under the counter'. Long queues were commonplace, often forming when the rumour spread that a delivery had been made. Very often when you eventually reached the head of the queue, the items that you had been queuing for had all gone.

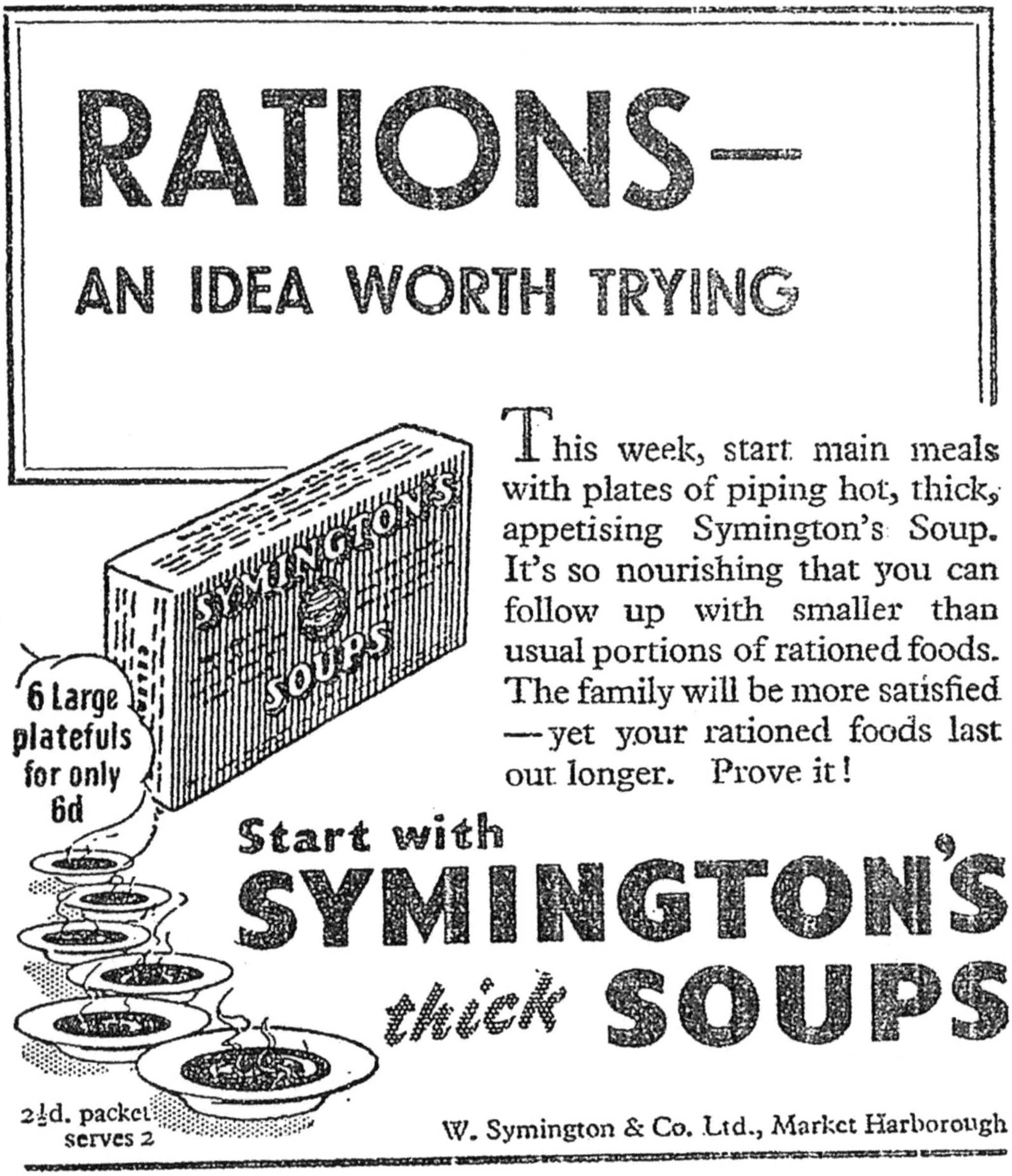

RATIONS –
AN IDEA WORTH TRYING

This week, start main meals with plates of piping hot, thick, appetising Symington's Soup. It's so nourishing that you can follow up with smaller than usual portions of rationed foods. The family will be more satisfied —yet your rationed foods last out longer. Prove it!

6 large platefuls for only 6d

Start with
SYMINGTON'S
thick SOUPS

2½d. packet serves 2

W. Symington & Co. Ltd., Market Harborough

With food shortages and rationing now in place, as in all other parts of the country, the inhabitants of Harpenden were encouraged to 'Dig for Victory'. This campaign introduced by the government called for every man and woman to keep an allotment, turn lawns and flower beds into vegetable gardens and, where possible, to keep chickens and rabbits.

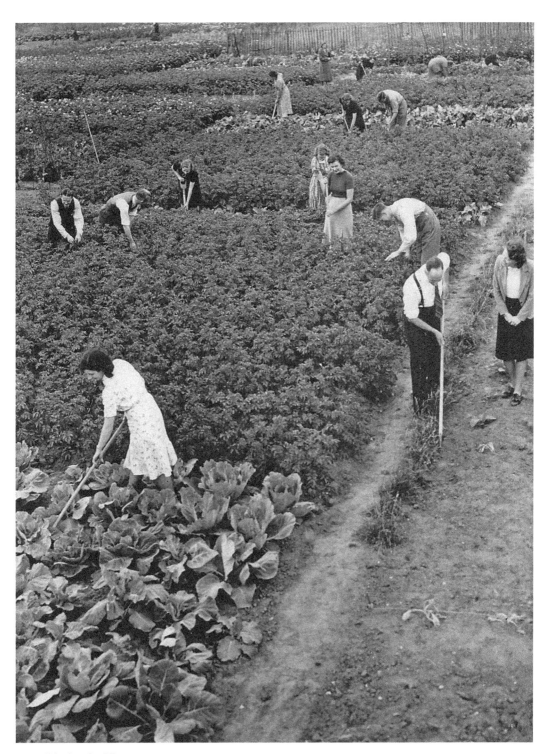

Digging for Victory.

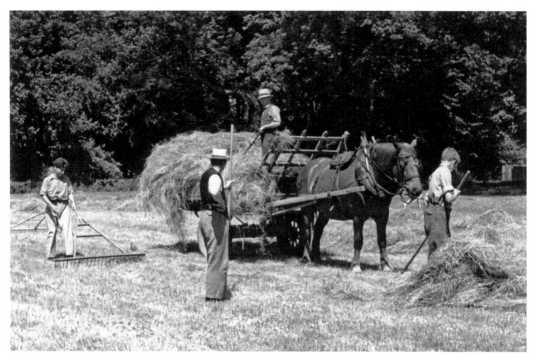

Harvesting, 1941

Many parts of Harpenden Common were also ploughed up to grow much-needed crops such as wheat and potatoes. With the absence of so many men of suitable age who were serving in the armed forces, the role of maintaining farms and helping to keep wartime Britain fed fell to a large extent on the Women's Land Army, better known as the Land Girls.

The WLA was started by the government in June 1939 where at first it asked for volunteers. This was later supplemented by conscription so that by 1944 it had over 80,000 members nationwide. The WLA lasted until its official disbandment on 21 October 1949.

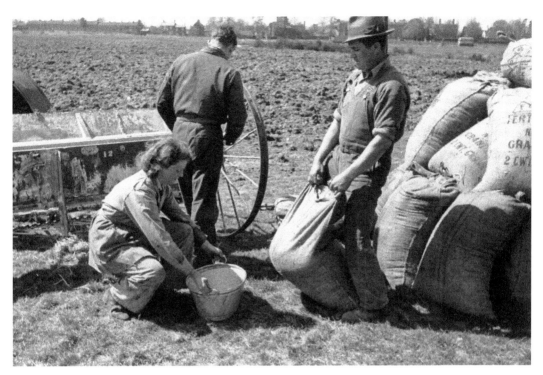

Spreading fertiliser, 1942.

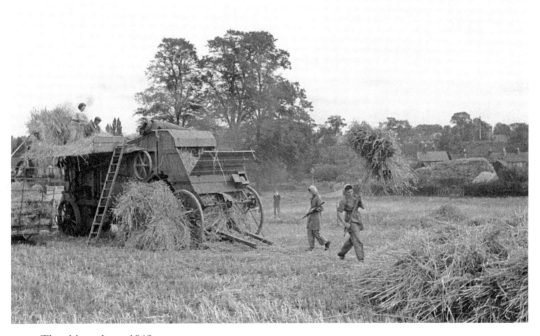

Threshing wheat, 1943.

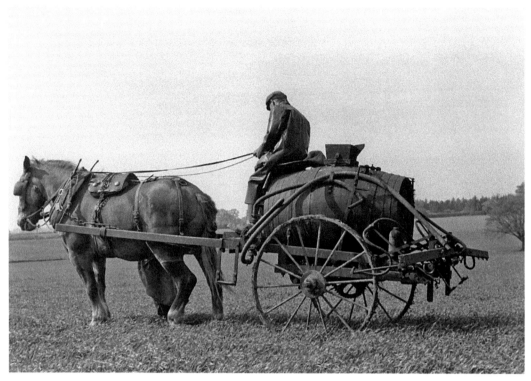

Spraying crops, 1944.

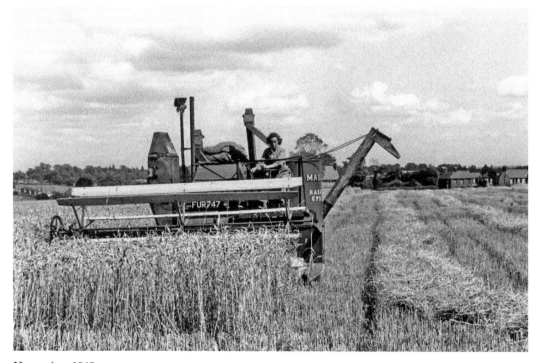

Harvesting, 1948.

Another commodity that was in dire need was scrap metal. In 1940, the council set up depots behind Bowers Parade and at their yard in Southdown Road to receive the multitude of decorative railings, chain-link fencing and an assortment of other metal items that could all be recycled for the war effort.

Aluminium too was eagerly sought after, with a great number of kitchen pots and pans and other utensils being collected, often by members of the Women's Voluntary Service (WVS). In the picture below members of a local ladies' committee are seen showing part of their collection to the chairman of the Urban District Council in the grounds of Harpenden Hall.

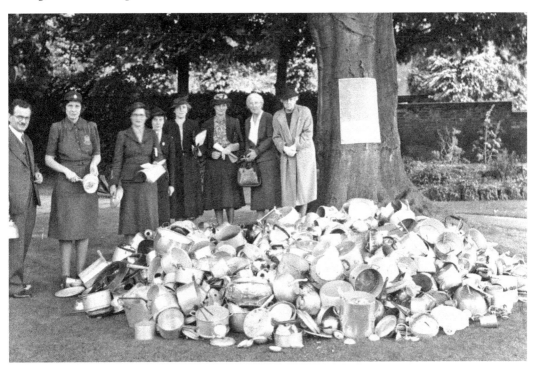

Aluminium collected for aircraft production.

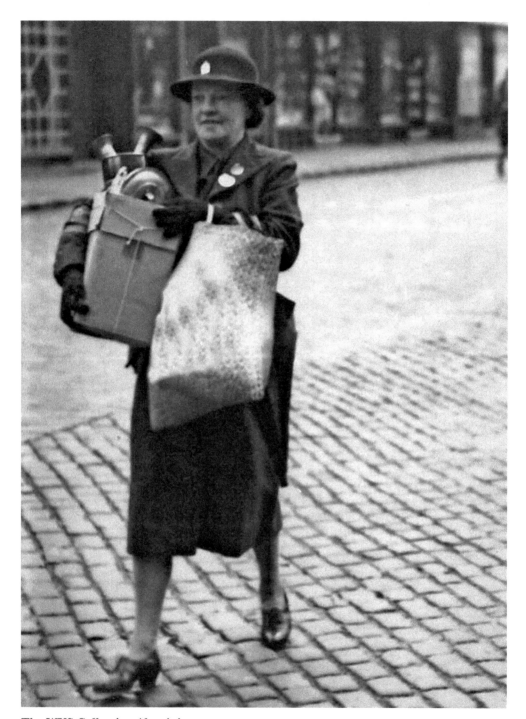

The WVS Collecting Aluminium
It is interesting to note that, with the number of empty houses and shops in the village at that time, many companies and organisations in London moved their businesses to the relative 'safety' of Harpenden. These included Century Insurance and Southern Life, the Bank of Adelaide and the Yugoslav Embassy, the latter occupying No. 53 Milton Road.

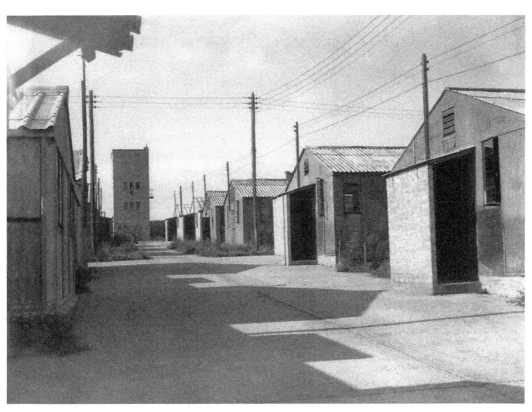

Batford Prisoner of War Camp After Final Repatriation, September 1948
Similar to many other places across Britain during the war, Harpenden had a prisoner of war camp (No. 95). This was located in the Batford area just south of Sauncy Wood, on the left-hand side of Common Lane, just before you reached Windmill Cottage as you headed in the direction of Mackerye End.

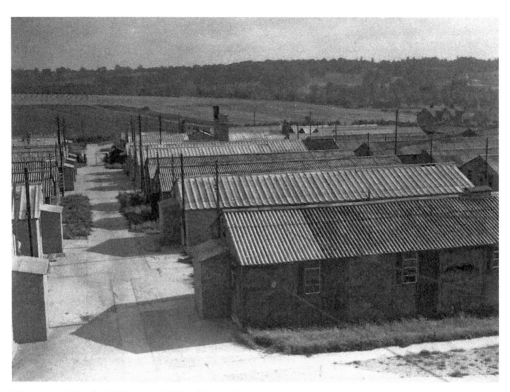

The vacated Batford Prisoner of War Camp, September 1948.

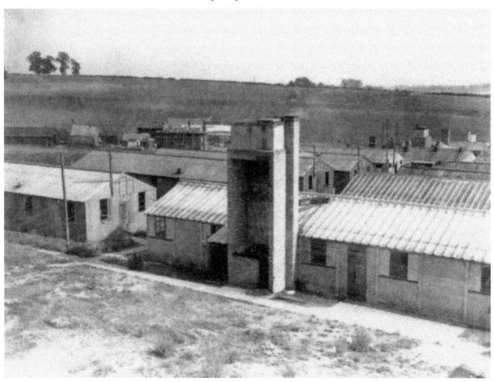

It was originally set up in May 1943 to house Italian prisoners, accommodating around 600 men. Initially, for the first few weeks accommodation and toilet arrangements were fairly basic, but gradually tents were replaced by huts, and the enlargement of the sewage system was eventually completed.

In October 1943, a peace treaty was signed between Italy and the Allies that altered the status of the Italians, who, although still prisoners, were granted better treatment and certain privileges. In July 1944, the status of the camp was changed to that of an Italian Labour Battalion Camp, with the internees able to be gainfully employed – mainly on farms in the locality.

During the following November, the Italians were moved out of the camp, some living in hostels with others remaining on the farms where they had worked. Following their departure, 750 German 'other ranks' prisoners (i.e. not officers) were incarcerated there until the repatriation programme was finally completed in July 1948.

After the war had ended and before their repatriation, the prisoners were allowed out of the camp on their own, either to work on the land or to be usefully occupied in a variety of manual tasks for the council, which during the winter months included clearing the snow and ice from the paths and pavements before returning to their quarters in the evening.

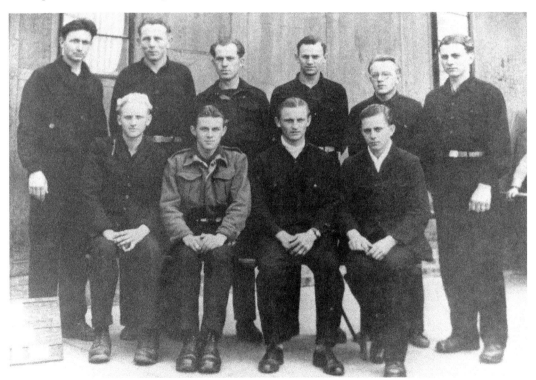

German prisoners of war at Batford POW Camp (No. 95).

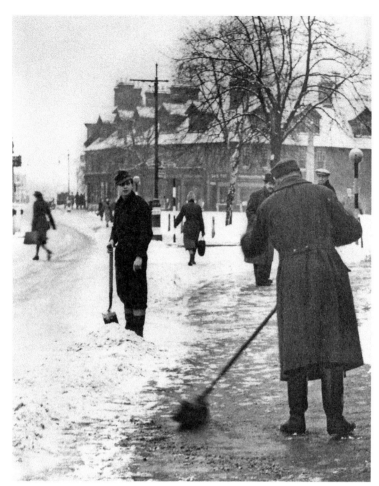

German POWs clearing
snow and ice from
the pavements in the
High Street, near
Church Green.

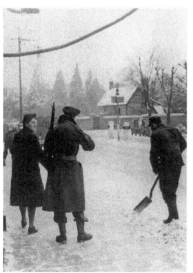

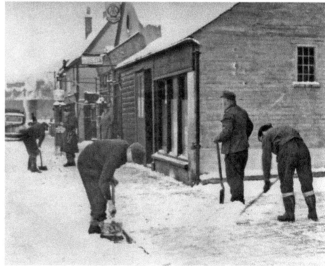

German POWs clearing snow in the High Street under armed guard.

With the war ending in May 1945, those prisoners with families who had hoped to return home almost immediately discovered for several reasons that repatriation would not be taking place for the foreseeable future. Germany was in a state of absolute chaos, and with no civilian government, was under military rule.

Also, with severe food and housing shortages, it was felt that until our servicemen had returned for demobilisation, the prisoners as a labour force could be utilised primarily in agriculture and the rebuilding programme.

Understandably, with repatriation, a considerable number of prisoners nationwide opted to remain in this country, many of them having lived in East Germany, which was now under the control of the Russians.

Repatriation started in September 1946 and was completed by July 1948. Harpenden Urban District Council then took over the camp, renovating the huts to accommodate two families in each hut, one at either end, to help with the dire shortage of housing that existed at that time.

There were no escapes from Batford Prisoner of War Camp, although a tunnel was later discovered in 1958 when the foundations for a new housing estate were being built. However, this was found to have been dug many years earlier to obtain chalk for mixing with the soil, a common agricultural practice in the area, rather than an escape tunnel.

Entertainment

Home life during those dark days of the Second World War revolved mostly around the wireless, which in the absence of television provided the main source of information and entertainment. Popular programmes included *ITMA*, which stood for *It's That Man Again* (a phrase often used in the media when referring to Adolf Hitler) and featured the Liverpudlian comedian Tommy Handley.

Other favourites were *Desert Island Discs* and *Music While You Work*, the latter being relayed via tannoy systems twice daily for half an hour in factories all over the country.

The cinema too attracted large audiences, the silver screen giving some much needed relief away from the world of rationing and air raids. However, as soon as the legend 'AIR RAID IN PROGRESS – YOU ARE ADVISED TO TAKE SHELTER' appeared, patrons were quickly brought back to reality and immediately left to take refuge in the nearest shelter.

Harpenden was indeed fortunate to have two cinemas, the Austral and the Regent. Before the war the latter had been a Methodist chapel. Films of the day included *Rebecca*, *Mrs Miniver* with Greer Garson, and the patriotic 1942 war film *In Which We Serve* directed and starring Noel Coward as Captain Kinross. *Gone with the Wind* with Clark Gable and Vivien Leigh was another popular film of the time.

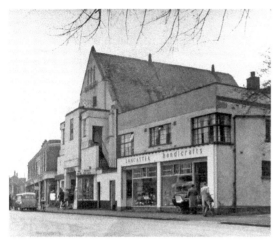

The Regent Cinema

The owner of the Regent was Mr L. D. Lattey. One interesting feature of the cinema was Murdoch, a little dog who had made his home in the foyer. Murdoch, a Sealyham, had been the cinema's mascot since the early days of the war when he had decided to take up residence there. The dog, which must have been the dirtiest, most intelligent and wiliest canine in the world, had belonged to an army officer who had been stationed in Harpenden, but when he had subsequently been posted Murdoch had remained in the cinema.

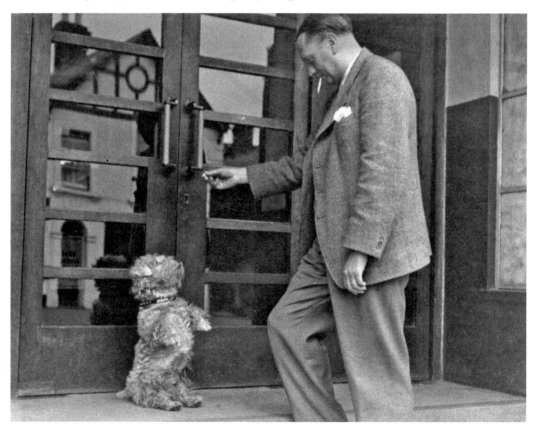

Murdoch with the owner of the Regent Cinema, Mr L. D. Lattey.

During those dark days of 1943, it would appear that even in Harpenden there was still the odd petty crime to contend with by the local police, as the following extract from a policeman's notebook confirms:

Robert John Gray (DEFT/1/1)
64, High Street
Harpenden

On Wednesday, 6th October, 1943, I went to the Regent Cinema, Harpenden. I left my pedal cycle against the rear wall of the cinema and last saw it at 6.20 pm.
I came out about 8.30 pm and found my cycle missing.
It is a gents BSA cycle, all black with 28" wheels No. W2 (262).
Has Dunlop Edinburgh on rear wheel and John Bull on front wheel.
Pull up brakes, rubber pedals and small bell on left handlebar.
3 speed with gear case. Battery lamps f & r

Cycle in good condition.
Value: £7.10s
Signature
20.50 6.10.43
P.C.281

The following extract from the diary states:

On Fri. 8th. Oct. I attended Harpenden Police Station where I was shown a pedal cycle which I identify (sic) as my property and the cycle which was stolen from the Regent Cinema, Harpenden on 6th. October, 1943.
Signature
Time & Date

Unfortunately, the report does not state how the cycle was recovered or whether it had been handed into the police station. It would appear that with such a speedy recovery, this was more than likely a theft by an opportunist quick to realise that here was an easy way to save the bus fare home. At least the hapless Robert John Gray was reunited with his bicycle again. Let's hope that the next time he frequented the Regent he made sure that he brought a strong padlock with him as well.

With the opening of the new Harpenden Public Hall in 1938, the weekly Saturday night dances were a 'must' for the local lads and girls, and especially the soldiers who were billeted in the village. American Army Air Force personnel would also drive from their camp at Bovingdon to jitterbug the night away, not always popularly received by the locals, and many was the time when the military police were needed to break up the odd fracas or two.

These weekly dances were a great morale booster, where for a few short hours the lights, music and company let you forget the austerity and the dangers of war. You could live your dreams in a make-believe world just like a 'Tinseltown' Hollywood film.

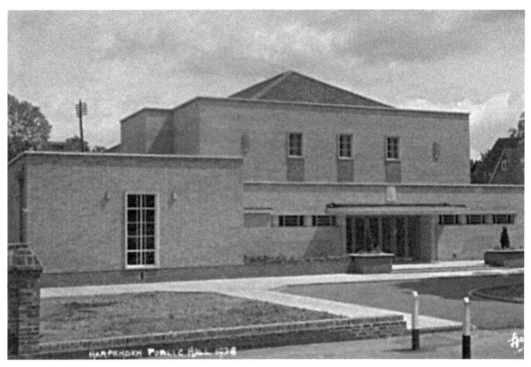

Harpenden Public Hall.

LOCAL DANCE ORGANISATIONS 23

ADMIT TO GRAND

CHARITY DANCE
AT THE
PUBLIC HALL, Southdown Road

EASTER MONDAY, APRIL 22nd, 1946
8-0 p.m. to 12 p.m.

MUSIC BY GEORGE MASON AND HIS BAND

H M FORCES 2/6   Buffet

IN AID OF LOCAL CHARITIES

Entry ticket to one of the Public Hall's popular post-war dances.

Chapter 4

Peace at Last

On Tuesday 8 May 1945 the long-awaited day that the whole country had prayed and longed for arrived – peacetime. This was Victory in Europe Day (VE Day), although it would be another three months before the war was finally over. When two hydrogen bombs were dropped on Hiroshima and Nagasaki, bringing victory with the war on Japan (VJ Day), nearly six years of hostilities had at last ended.

German forces had signed an unconditional surrender the previous morning – 7 May – but the Allied leaders agreed to wait until 3 p.m. BST on 8 May before making an official announcement so that simultaneous declarations could be made from London, Washington and Moscow.

Following Prime Minister Winston Churchill's announcement that 8 May was designated a public holiday, people from all over the country, including Harpenden, came out onto the streets in joyous celebration. Church bells rang out, schools closed and there was a palpable buzz of excitement and happiness as the residents prepared their own festivities as, like numerous communities in and around the village, huge bonfires were swiftly erected.

Although food was in very short supply, by pooling the meagre rations that were available a 'sumptuous' buffet was produced by the ladies for the evening frivolities, with the men taking care of the liquid refreshments. In some areas, music was provided on old wind-up gramophones and with the strains of Vera Lynn merging with the sounds of laughter and loud chatter, accompanied by the clink of beer glasses, VE Day was finally over and the peace in all of its austerity was about to begin.

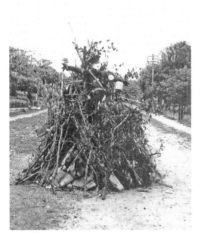 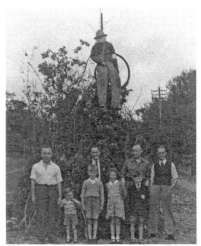

A typical Victory bonfire.

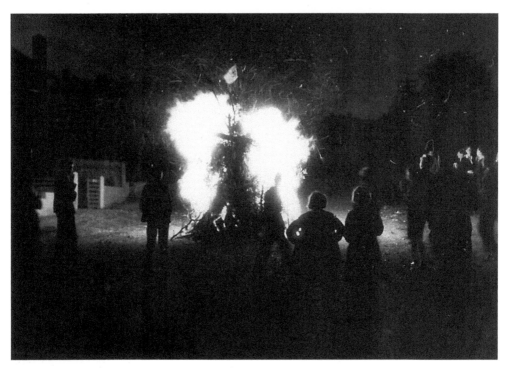

VE night celebrations.

THE EMBASSY OF THE UNION OF SOVIET SOCIALIST REPUBLICS

Request the pleasure of your company

at the first showing of

The Full-Length Documentary Films :

"BERLIN"

and

"THE VICTORY PARADE IN MOSCOW"

at the

LEICESTER SQUARE CINEMA, LEICESTER SQUARE, W.C.1

on WEDNESDAY, 5th SEPTEMBER, 1945

at 7.30 p.m.

An invitation from the embassy of the USSR to the first screening in 1945 of two documentary films entitled *Berlin* and *The Victory Parade in Moscow*.

Chapter 5

Post-War Celebrations

During those drab post-war years of the late 1940s and early 1950s, one of the attractions that was always eagerly looked forward to in Harpenden was the arrival of the funfair.

Several times a year the area adjacent to the Silver Cup Pond was transformed as an assortment of merry-go-rounds and stalls were assembled in preparation for the bank holiday weekend. It was always a popular venue and people from miles around would converge on the Common to enjoy the various rides and stalls at *6d* a go.

As well as all the enjoyment of those bank holidays, there was always the additional treat of the Statute Fair, or 'Stattie' as it was more popularly known, that came to the village for two weekdays every September. This annual event was much larger than the usual bank holiday fairs. It originated in bygone days when it was also called a hiring fair, where local employers had the opportunity to choose and recruit additional labour such as farm workers, domestic servants or artisans. Once agreement had been reached, the employer would give his new worker a small sum of money to spend among the stalls set up at the fair. These days though the event is purely for pleasure only.

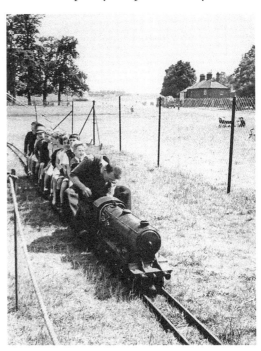

A miniature steam train on Harpenden Common.

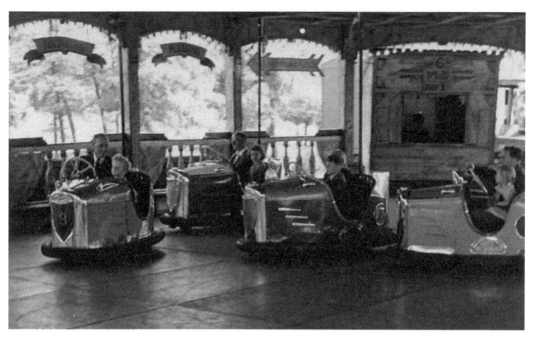

All the fun of the fair!

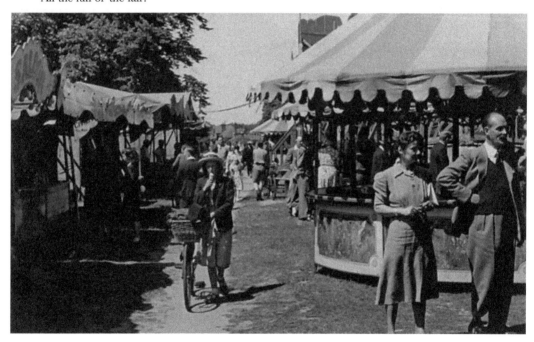

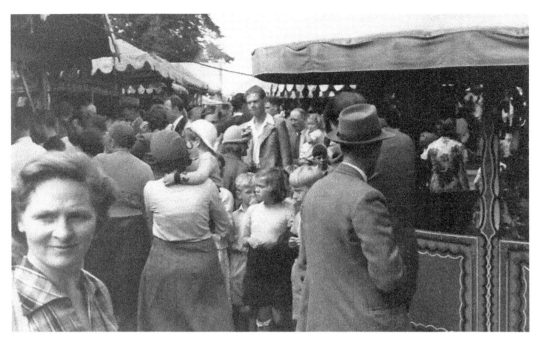

Enjoying a bank holiday weekend.

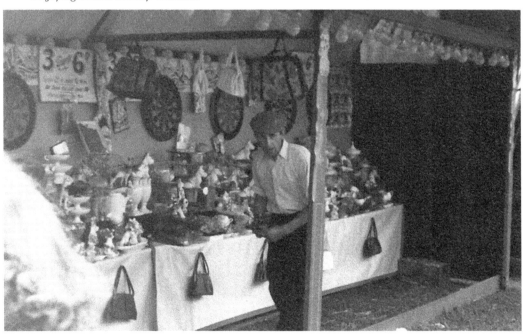

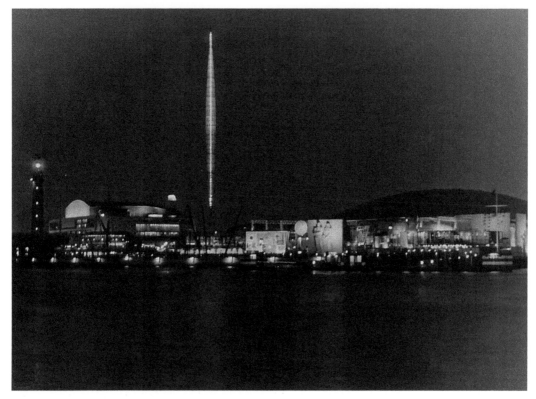

The Skylon, Festival of Britain, 1951

One event that was destined to bring some much-needed colour and excitement to an otherwise drab and lacklustre country, where post-war recovery was slow and rationing was still very much in evidence, was the Festival of Britain in 1951.

Whit Monday, 14 May, was a bank holiday and although it wasn't raining it was cloudy and somewhat cool. Harpenden, in common with Festival of Britain celebrations being held all around the country, had organised a glittering programme of festivities and events for the enjoyment of both residents and visitors alike over the next six days.

That year of 1951 was a festival year for Britain, to mark 100 years of progress since 1851 when the Crystal Palace, latterly destroyed by fire, was built in Hyde Park, London, in order to stage a Great Exhibition to show the world what Britain had achieved. Now, a hundred years later, with the generosity of a few public-spirited people and the enthusiasm of the residents, Harpenden was ready to rightly take her place in the 1951 Festival of Britain celebrations.

In London, on a 27-acre site on the South Bank, the great Dome of Discovery and the futuristic Skylon, apparently suspended with no visible means of support over the Festival Gardens at Battersea, gave some reassurance that the austerity and shortages of the war and post-war years were finally starting to disappear. This was the sign that there was indeed hope for the future.

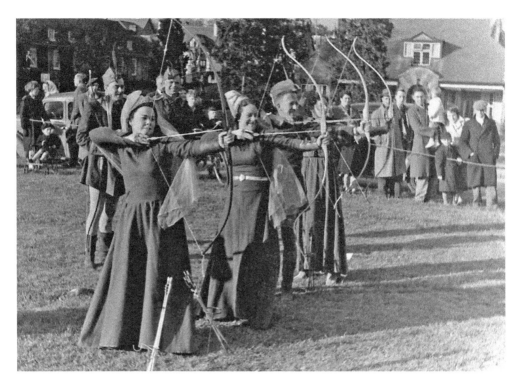

Old-time Sports on the Common

Back in Harpenden, at precisely 11 a.m., a peal of bells from the parish church opened the week of revels, and what a week it was. Most of the events that took place each day started either in the late afternoon or early evening. Old-time sports including archery and tennis were very popular, with each of the participants dressed in period costume. There was quite a bit of friendly banter between the opposing teams, especially those playing croquet, where rules were thrown to the wind and a considerable amount of cheating took place, much to the delight of the spectators.

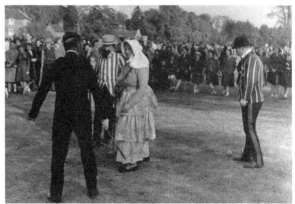

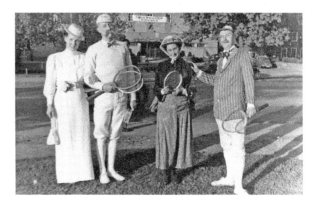

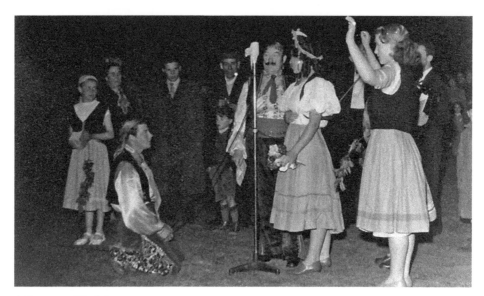

A Romany Wedding

As the week of revels progressed, the crowds of onlookers were given the privilege of witnessing a gypsy wedding that had been arranged by Gypsy Petulengro, the King of the Romanies. This took place on the Common in the glow and darting shadows of a mammoth camp fire that had been lit for the occasion. With the bridal party in traditional dress and the haunting strains of soft gypsy music, it was a fascinating spectacle to behold. The Romany couple stood before Petulengro swearing 'to let no other have a place in their hearts until death'. He then cut their hands so that the blood mingled, joining the bridegroom's right and the bride's left with a silken cord in which knots of affection, sincerity, long life, fidelity and the blessing of fertility had been tied by the bridesmaids. With the cord then cut, the bridegroom jumped across a small fire, closely followed by his bride, the happy couple then returning together hand in hand.

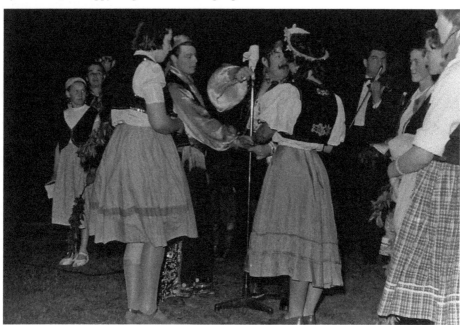

The following Saturday was the culmination of a wonderful week of celebrations, starting with a grand carnival procession of decorated agricultural and trade vehicles, private cars and tableaux that assembled in Leyton Road for the eleven o'clock start, with crowds already gathering along the route. Led by 'John Bull' on horseback, the procession proceeded across Church Green to Lower High Street, up Vaughan Road, along Victoria Road to Station Road and back again along the High Street.

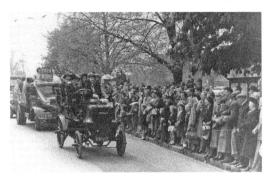 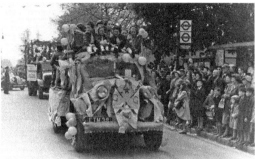

The carnival procession wending its way out of Station Road and into the High Street.

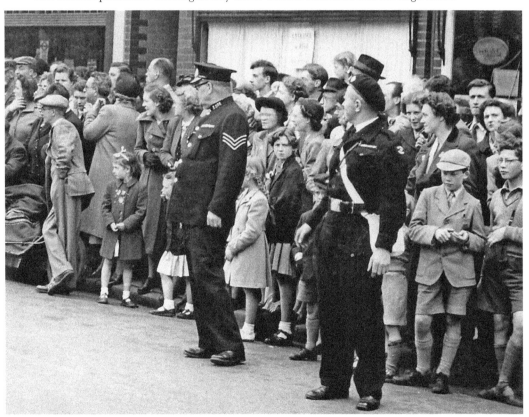

Some of the crowd waiting for the procession to pass.

Judging took place en route, with the lucky winners parading separately through the High Street after the awards had been made. This brought forth much applause and cheering from the happy onlookers, sometimes three or four deep in places on the pavement. One of the spectators' favourites on that memorable day was the marching and counter-marching through the High Street of the band of HM Life Guards. For a short while the stirring marches of Safroni and Holzmann lifted the spirits making the spellbound crowds momentarily forget the deprivation and shortages that were still in evidence. It was sheer magic while it lasted.

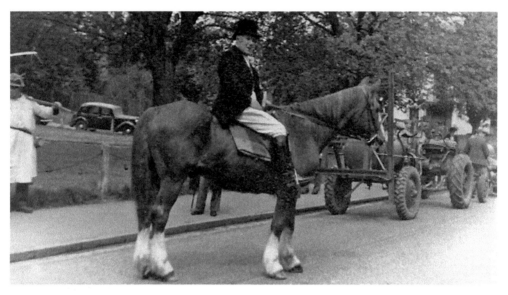

Above: 'John Bull' on horseback in Leyton Green.

Left: The 'Olde Chariot'.

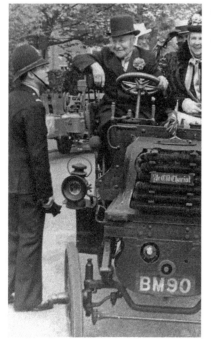

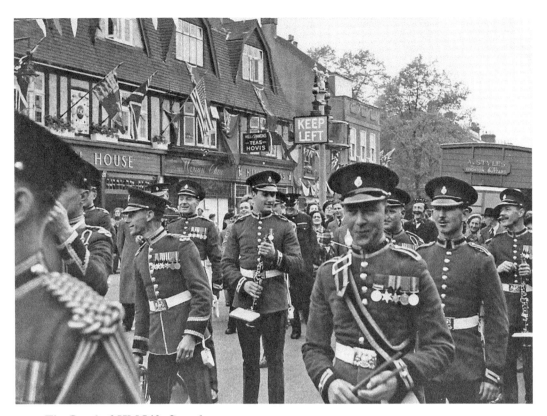

The Band of HM Life Guards

The entertainment and displays went on and on without any respite. There were barrel races for the men, perambulator races for the women, hoop races for the girls and soapbox trolley races for the boys. Punch and Judy on the High Street greens attracted a large audience of mesmerised youngsters, and there was a display by the Legion of Frontiersmen on the Common. There were maypole and children's dancing, ventriloquists, conjurers and jugglers on the greens and a service of church music in the Parish Church at six o'clock. A children's fair in Rothamsted Park did a roaring business throughout the afternoon.

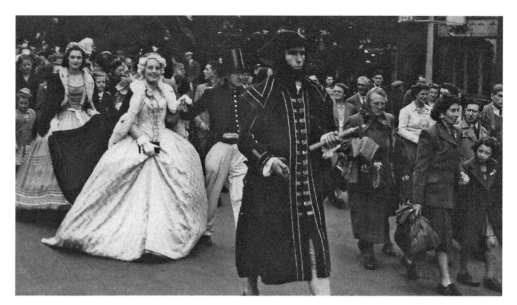

The Carnival Queen

As the afternoon turned to evening and dusk started to descend, illuminations with fairy lights and Oriental lanterns were switched on. The parish church and Harpenden Hall were floodlit too. The whole panorama was that of an enchanted wonderland. During the evening there was a floral dance through the village followed by folk dancing on the Common led by the Hertfordshire Folk Dance Society.

At nine o'clock, Harpenden Fire Service gave a superb display with illuminations near the Silver Cup Pond. One of their popular items was a game of 'football' played with a ball on the water and hoses at each end of the pond. This was followed by the grand finale: a fantastic display of fireworks on the Common that seemed to go on forever. It was absolutely superb. What a glittering end to the most action-packed and exciting of weeks.

Following the death of George VI on 6 February 1952 and the proclamation that we now had a new monarch, Elizabeth II, Harpenden was again preparing for another week of celebrations to mark the coronation, the date of which had been set for Tuesday 2 June 1953.

As coronation day dawned, the bells rang out from the parish church to proclaim the start of the new Elizabethan age and of the celebrations that were to follow. And what a varied programme there was too, with 'Fairyland' being the central theme.

Despite the miserable cold weather and torrential showers of rain that unfortunately curtailed a lot of the outside activities, the organisers' swift changeover to the alternative programme ensured that many of the arrangements could still take place in the various halls. Throngs of happy people crowded into the Public Hall for the United Service of Thanksgiving and to watch the live television broadcast of the coronation on several strategically placed sets that enabled everybody to get a good view.

All seats in the hall were taken, with many people standing at the back and round the sides. No sooner had the transmission finished and the Public Hall had emptied, than hundreds of excited children dressed in brightly coloured fancy dress costumes trooped in to enjoy all the fun of a large tea party. For those with a musical ear, one could sit and relax listening to the Light Operatic Society singing excerpts from Gilbert and Sullivan in the Methodist Church Hall. There was something to appeal to everyone, from the young to the not so young. At the end of that day of pageantry and splendour that we had witnessed on our television sets, following the illumination of Fairyland in the village, a beacon was lit on the Common. What a spectacular end to the most exciting of days.

Over the next few evenings, there was an absolute feast of entertainment to suit the most discerning of tastes. Elizabethan sports were very popular, with Cornish wrestling, comic bear-baiting, sword play, archery and hurling to name but a few. For those who enjoyed dancing, the glittering Coronation Ball was held in the Public Hall on the Friday, with the highlight of the evening being the arrival of the Fairy Queen in her coach.

MORNING

10 o'clock.	MAYPOLE and CHILDREN'S DANCING on the Common. TOWN CRIER, JESTER, MINSTRELS, etc. (and throughout the afternoon).
10.30 o'clock.	The BAND of H.M. LIFE GUARDS will attend by kind permission of Colonel F. F. B. St. George (Commanding Household Cavalry). Director of Music—Lt.-Col. A. Lemoine, p.s.m.
11 o'clock.	GRAND CARNIVAL PROCESSION of FAIRIES and TABLEAUX and other INNOVATIONS of the MORTALS, including Cycles, Private Cars, Trade Vehicles, etc.

> The Procession will assemble at 10.30 o'clock in Leyton Road and will proceed via Church Green, High Street, Vaughan Road, Victoria Road, Station Road, and back along the High Street. JUDGING will take place en route and the WINNERS will later parade separately through the High Street.

12 midday.	PRESENTATION of AWARDS on the Common.
12.30 o'clock.	CLOWNS, VENTRILOQUIST, CONJURER, etc. (and throughout the afternoon).

AFTERNOON

2 o'clock.	RACES through the HIGH STREET, with Barrels, Hoops and other impedimenta. CHILDREN'S FAIR in Rothamsted Park (throughout the afternoon).
2.45 o'clock.	DISPLAYS on the Common:— BOADICEA, by residents of Batford. ELIZABETH I, by the Townswomen's Guild. "TUDOR ROSE," by the combined Women's Institutes. VICTORIA, by members of the National Children's Home. ELIZABETH II, by the National Council of Women.

4 o'clock.	DISPLAYS by local DANCING SCHOOLS (on the Common and on the Greens). GILBERT AND SULLIVAN, by the Light Operatic Society (on High Street Green). SHAKESPEARE in a GARDEN, by the Drama League (in the Grounds of St. Dominic's Convent).
5 o'clock.	"CHANGING OF THE BANDS" (on the Common).

> The Band of H.M. LIFE GUARDS will be relieved by the CENTRAL BAND of the ROYAL AIR FORCE (MILITARY BAND), which will continue until the end of the proceedings. The Central Band will attend by kind permission of the Air Council, conducted by Wing Commander A. E. Sims, O.B.E., L.R.A.M., A.R.C.M., Organising Director of Music, Royal Air Force.

EVENING

6 o'clock.	SQUARE DANCING and COUNTRY DANCING (through the Village and on the Common)
7 o'clock.	Repeat Performances of SHAKESPEARE and GILBERT AND SULLIVAN.
8 o'clock.	ASSEMBLY of the ORDER OF CHIVALRY (on the Common). "MAGNA CARTA," with innovations.
9 o'clock.	STAGE COACH and HIGHWAYMEN. DANCE in the Public Hall (tickets 4s. each, obtainable from Thorn, The Tobacconist, High Street).
9.30 o'clock.	PROCESSION of DECORATED and ILLUMINATED CARS, etc., around the Village.
10.30 o'clock. to 11.30 o'clock.	GRAND FIREWORK DISPLAY (on the Common) by Brocks "Crystal Palace" Fireworks Ltd.

God Save the Queen

Coronation Programme of Events

As the sun came out that Saturday morning, the final day of the celebrations, so did the crowds in their hundreds to enjoy over thirteen hours of non-stop entertainment. The day started with a carnival procession of decorated trade vehicles and private cars that formed up outside the Regent Cinema in Leyton Road and stretched right back to the Silver Cup public house. Lorries and cars were laden with ingenious and artistic decorations of all descriptions, one even bearing a model of The Mall complete with the coronation coach, on which many hours of painstaking work had obviously been lavished.

The band of HM Life Guards, making a welcome return to Harpenden, led the procession around the same route that the festival tableaux had travelled two years earlier to the cheers and applause of the happy crowds. The presentation of awards was later given to the lucky and well-deserved winners on the Common.

During the afternoon, which had now turned warm and sunny, there were various races along the High Street as the Life Guards played selections in the forecourt of The George pub. Later, Queen Boadicea came charging up from Southdown in her chariot leading a party of ancient Britons into a pitched battle with a unit of well-trained Roman soldiers. The outcome wasn't all that clear but at least the participants seemed to enjoy themselves, with the cheering crowd giving enthusiastic encouragement to their chosen side.

As the revelry continued into the evening, there was square dancing and country dancing through the village and on the Common, and performances of Shakespeare and Gilbert and Sullivan. The finale to this glittering week of festivities was a procession of decorated and illuminated cars along the High Street that was followed by a grand firework display on the Common.

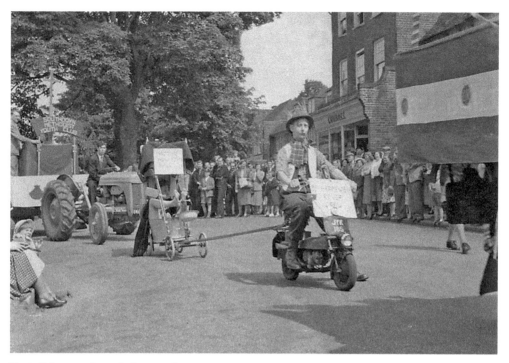

Part of the grand carnival procession.

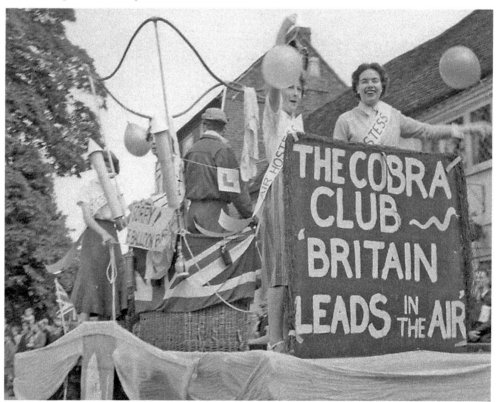

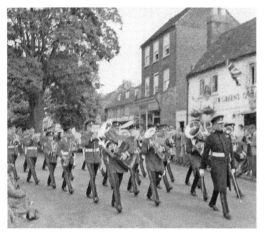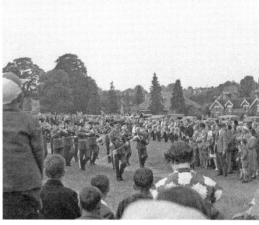

The band passing the Cross Keys public house before their arrival on the Common.

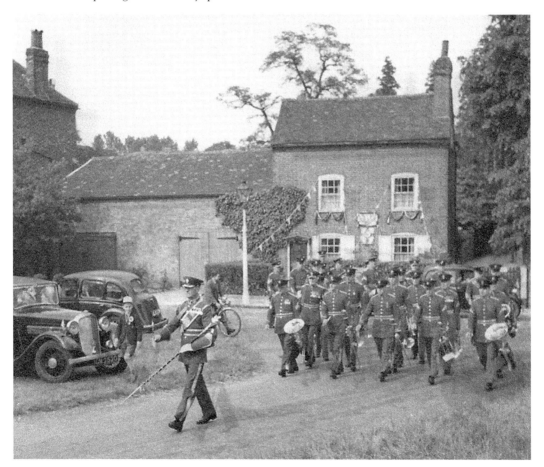

The band's arrival on the Common.

Chapter 6

The Post-War Years of the 1950s, '60s and '70s

As the austerity and drabness of the immediate post-war years of the late 1940s and early 1950s gradually started to recede and memories of wartime faded into history, we see the village develop into the charming town that we know today, and witness some of the iconic views recorded for posterity taken during the late 1950s, 1960s and 1970s.

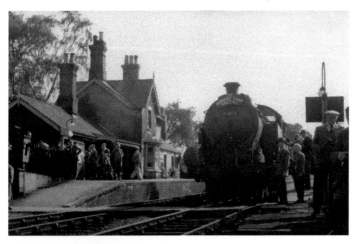

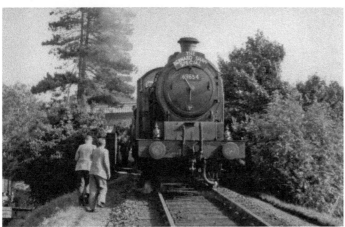

The Bernard Shaw Special
Throngs of excited people and enthusiasts line the platform as *The Bernard Shaw Special* pulls into Harpenden East station on the Great Northern Railway branch line in the 1950s. The train, pulled by Engine No. 69654, was one of a series of day excursions that ran from either Elephant & Castle or Clapham Junction in London to Harpenden via Wheathampstead. The many devotees of renowned Irish playwright George Bernard Shaw alighted to head for Shaw's Corner, now part of the National Trust, at nearby Ayot St Lawrence, the home of the great man. He lived there until his death at the age of ninety-four on 2 November 1950.

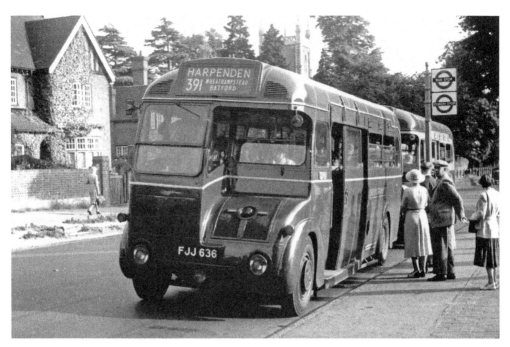

Public Transport

On 28 June 1952, the 391 bus service (above) is preparing to depart from St Albans for its journey through Wheathampstead and Batford to its destination at Church Green, Harpenden. This TF class of London Transport single-decker bus was introduced just prior to the Second World War, during which they were utilised on ambulance work, and would have had longer service lives had not the RF class bus replaced them in the 1950s. Note the radiator built into the distinctive curved nearside front wing. Below is a London Transport single-decker that used to travel between Harpenden and Batford in the early 1960s. Bus RW2, an AEC Reliance with a Willowbrook body, was one of three similar buses bought by London Transport.

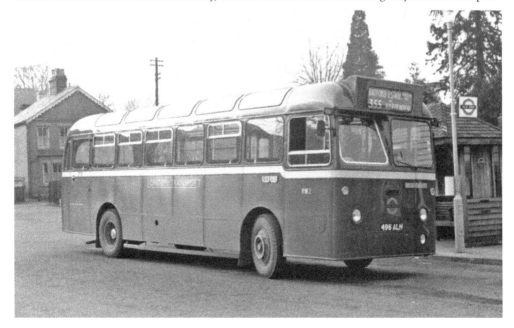

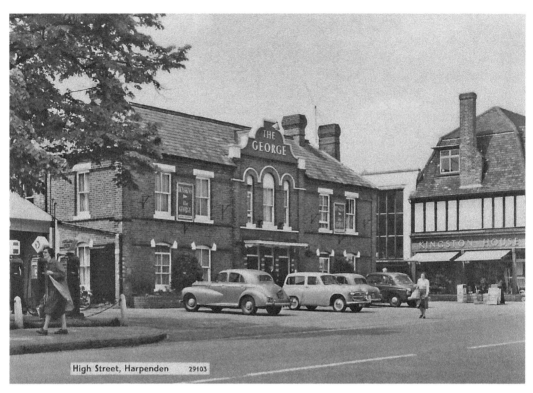

High Street, Harpenden 29103

The George Hotel and Kingston House.

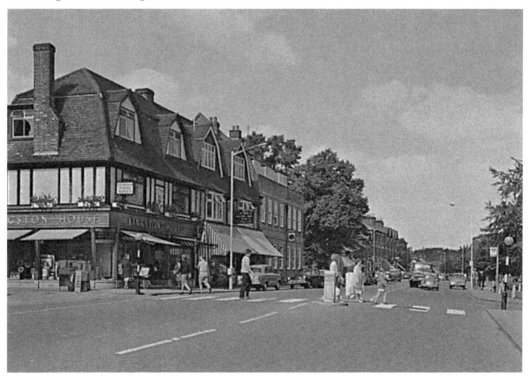

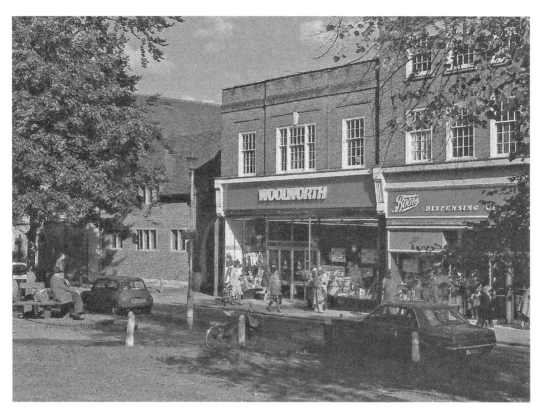

Lower High Street.

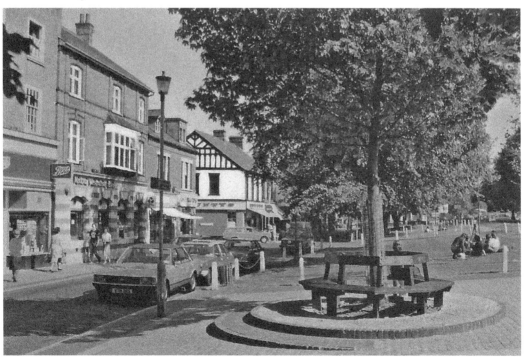

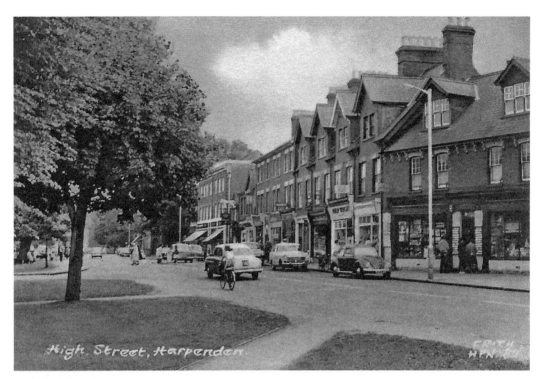

The High Street.

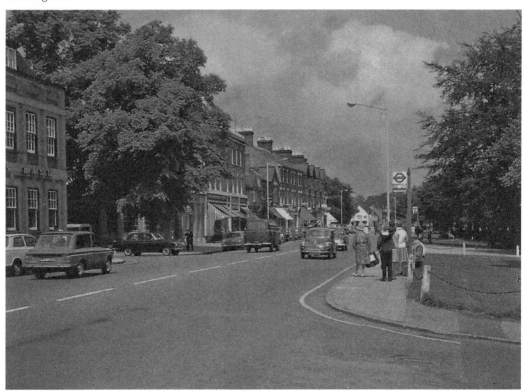

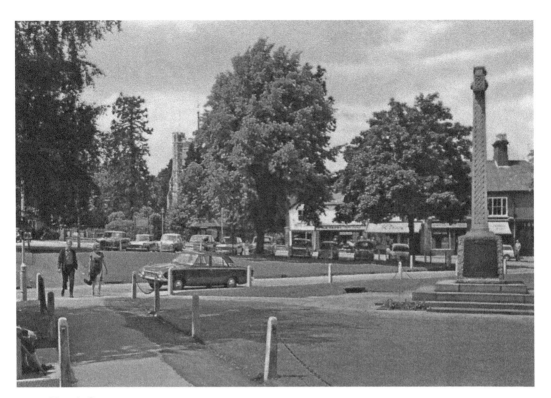

Church Green.

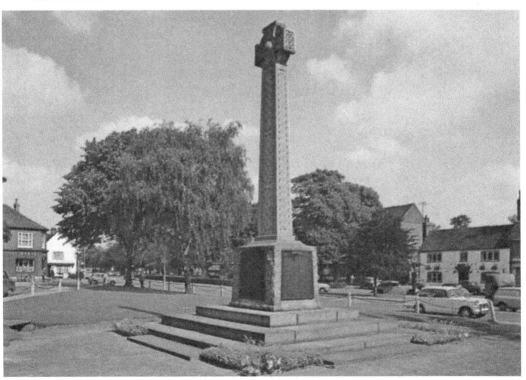

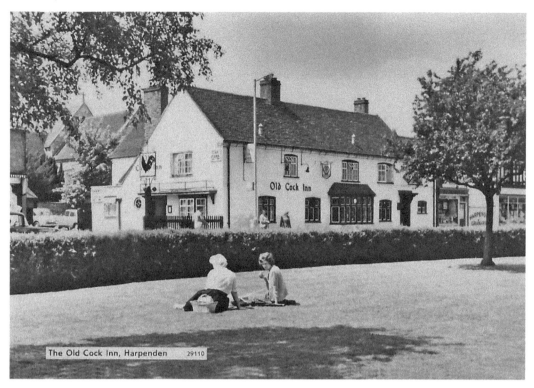

The Old Cock Inn and the Harpenden coronation commemoration sign.

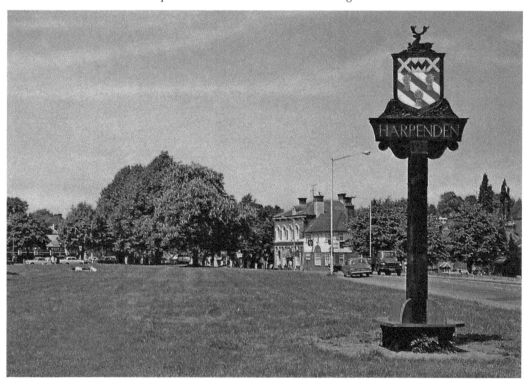

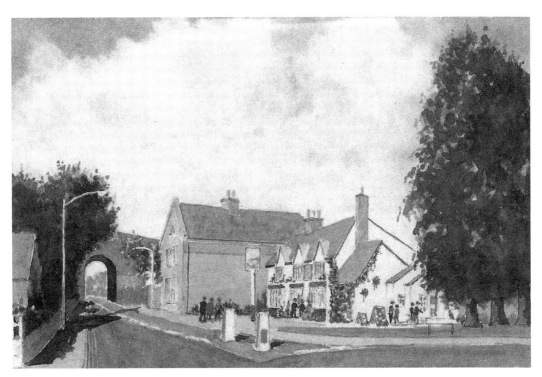

Southdown and Pimlico Place, West Common.

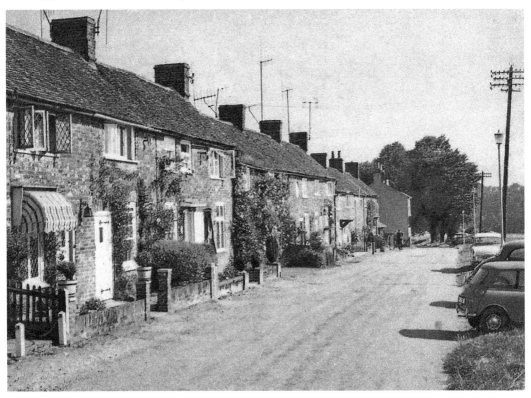

Acknowledgements

I am indebted to the following: Archaeological Services & Consultancy Ltd; Christine Barrow, the Pilkington Family Trust; Building Research Establishment; Harpenden Cricket Club; Fenella Lattey; Rosemary Ross, Harpenden & District Local History Society; the late Richard Todd, OBE; Tim Wales, MCLIP FHEA FRSA, Rothamsted Research and Watford Central Library.

Special thanks are extended to my wife Betty for her constant support, encouragement and invaluable input, to my son Mark for his continuous IT support and to my publisher for their kind assistance in producing this book.

Every endeavour has been made to contact all copyright holders and any errors that have occurred are inadvertent. Anyone who for any reason has not been contacted is invited to write to the publishers so that a full acknowledgement may be made in any subsequent edition of this book.

The images on the following pages are courtesy of H&DLHS: 7, 10, 13, 15, 16, 18, 72, 73, 75, 80, 81, 83, 95, 97, 98 and 99. The image on page 102 is courtesy of Fenella Lattey. Images on pages 92, 93 and 94 are copyright Lawes Agricultural Trust/Rothamsted Research.